golden steps to
inner peace,
happiness &
enlightenment

golden steps to
inner peace, happiness & enlightenment

How to heal your life, find love and happiness,
and reach enlightenment in this lifetime.

Mildred Ryan

the columba press

First published in 2015 by
The Columba Press
55A Spruce Avenue
Stillorgan Industrial Park
Blackrock, Co. Dublin

ISBN 9781782182351

Cover and layout design by Helene Pertl | The Columba Press
Cover photograph © iStock
Origination by The Columba Press

To my mother, for giving so much.
There aren't enough ways to thank you.

To my sister Deirdre, for your kindness,
generosity and deep wisdom.

To my brother Declan, for always being willing
to give a helping hand.

To my dad, your kindness and gentleness
will be in our hearts forever.

Sending you lots of love.

Included with the Book

 Five free guided meditations in MP3 format which you can listen to or download.

There are many healing exercises throughout the book. All the healing journeys are written with detailed instructions for you to follow so that you can gain the most benefit. Of course, the best way to take a healing journey is to be guided through the whole process. So I have recorded five guided meditations, and am offering the recordings as free gifts to accompany this book.

The guided meditations are:
1. Fifteen minute relaxation—to refresh your mind, body and spirit.
2. Merge with your Higher Self—the light of your soul.
3. Golden Angelic Cloak of Light.
4. Oval of Heavenly Light—an experience of enlightenment.
5. DNA Healing—cleanse and reprogramme your DNA with new life and energy.

To listen to the recordings, or download the MP3 files, go to www.mildredryan.com/free-gifts

My vision

My vision for this book is that it will empower all who read it to know that they can find inner peace, love and happiness and reach enlightenment in this lifetime.

We are living in exciting times where the possibilities for growth and expansion are enormous.

I hope that through this book you will find all you need to step forward into your full potential and create the life you want to live — full of lightness, joy, love, abundance, peace, harmony and fulfilment; all the golden qualities of enlightenment.

I wish you many blessings as you take each golden step of your journey.

 Mildred

Contents

Included with the Book vi
My vision vii

INTRODUCTION 1
My journey to enlightenment 6
How this book came about 7
Enlightenment 9
A word of encouragement as you start on this journey 13
How to use this book 16

Section 1

LOVE AND JOY ARE THE KEYS TO ENLIGHTENMENT

Love 20
Living joyfully 29

Section 2

LIGHT UP YOUR LIFE

Blessings 42
Appreciation 46
Gratitude 49
A bright start to your day 52
Look for the gift in challenging situations 55
See the best in everyone 60
Divine communication 62
Creating abundance 68

Section 3

A CONSTANT SOURCE OF LOVE AND SUPPORT

Your Higher Self 72
Angels will light your way 81
Saints and Ascended Masters 87
A team to support you 89

Section 4

SPIRITUAL PRACTICE

Meditation 94
Prayers and inspirational words 98
Creating a safe and sacred environment for your
spiritual practice 100

Section 5

TRANSFORMATION AND SPIRITUAL GROWTH

Step into your power 104
Self-worth and confidence 107
Transform old habits and patterns 111
Forgiveness 115
Cutting cords 123
Disconnect from the collective consciousness 127
Cleansing with the Violet Flame 129

Section 6

HEALING ON ALL LEVELS

Healing 138
Cleanse and refresh your aura 142
Self-care 144
The power of thoughts 149

Clear mind chatter and circling thoughts 152
Worries, fears and negative emotions 154
The present moment 157

Section 7

HIGHER HEALING

Oval of heavenly light 160
DNA healing 166

Section 8

THE HEALING GIFTS OF NATURE

The healing gifts of nature 176
Love and kindness for animals 180
Dolphins—the angels of the ocean 191

Section 9

YOU CAN LIGHT UP THE WORLD

An Ambassador for the Light 196
Creating Heaven on Earth 198
Golden communities 200
Golden footsteps 203
Rays of divine light 204

Section 10

YOUR GOLDEN STEPS TO INNER PEACE, HAPPINESS AND
ENLIGHTENMENT

Your golden steps 208
Summary of the golden steps 209
About the author 215
Gratitude 217

Introduction

 This book will transform your life and the lives of others. It is a step-by-step guide to heal your life, find love and happiness and reach enlightenment in this lifetime.

MY WISH FOR YOU

This book outlines golden steps you can take to reach enlightenment and fill your heart with love, joy and peace. It offers guidance, wisdom, and lots of practical encouragement and suggestions, helping to put many things into practice so you can achieve your goal.

My wish for you is that reading this book will guide you on your path to a richer, more fulfilling, loving and joyous life. I hope that you will feel empowered to step forward into your full potential, push through any limitations and old ways of being, and become all you can be.

With each golden step you take, you will draw your own deep wisdom to the surface, enabling you to remember once again the magnificence of who you are.

This is a book of empowerment, growth and expansion.

The truths within this book are guided by my own personal journey towards enlightenment and spiritual growth, and inspiration received over many years of writing and teaching about spirituality. I have been divinely guided to share this information with others as a 'fast track' process towards gaining inner peace and enlightenment.

Do you want to reach enlightenment in this lifetime? The opportunity is available to you. This incredible time we live in, where many cosmic dispensations and energetic frequencies are being granted to Earth from the spiritual realms, allows for greater opportunities for spiritual advancement than ever before.

I hope the simplicity and truth of the words contained in this book will speak to your heart and soul. I hope it guides your passion and wisdom to create the life of your dreams—filled with love, joy, peace, abundance, harmony and fulfilment. These are the qualities that allow the light of your soul to shine radiantly, so that you can become an enlightened being.

This is a book for everyone, whatever your religion or beliefs. It contains universal truths which you can apply to all areas of your life to enhance your own spiritual practice.

 Love is the central theme—loving yourself, others and our planet Earth.

YOUR GOLDEN STEPS

The process of reaching a state of inner peace, happiness and enlightenment is fully explained within this book. It is a step-by-step journey, and each golden step you take will move you further along on your pathway to reach your goal.

The ten central sections of this book expand on different themes of how to create more love, joy and peace in your life.

SECTION I
— Living with love and joy in your heart.
These are two of the most important qualities to foster as you take each golden step towards inner peace, happiness and enlightenment.

SECTION 2

— Enlightening gems of wisdom.

These gems will light up your life, create golden opportunities,
and clear your pathway to enlightenment.

SECTION 3

— Stilling your mind and meditating.

Many methods are given, along with the beauty of prayer and
inspirational words.

SECTION 4

— Tools for transformation and spiritual growth.

These include confidence building, letting go of old habits
and patterns, and transforming troubling situations with love
and healing.

SECTION 5

— Steps for healing on all levels.

The focus is balancing mind, body and spirit.

SECTION 6

— Higher healing exercises.

This section offers exercises to help you expand your consciousness and accelerate spiritual growth.

SECTION 7

— Sources of love and support.

Guidelines are given on the constant source of love and support
that you can call on to assist you on your journey.

SECTION 8

— Mother Nature.

The healing gifts of Mother Nature, dolphins and our relationship with all life forms are explored in this section.

SECTION 9

— Becoming an Ambassador for the Light.

This explores how you can prepare to create Heaven on Earth
as you spread love, peace and harmony around you.

SECTION 10

— Your own personal plan.

Create your own golden steps to inner peace, happiness and enlightenment in this section.

THE BENEFITS OF TAKING THIS JOURNEY

You will be empowered to expand into your full potential, become all you can be, and create more Heaven on a daily basis in your life.

You will be guided to clear out old issues and patterns holding you back, so you are free to move forward and create the life of your dreams.

Remember, this journey is taken step by step. As you take each step, the next step is revealed to you.

My aim in writing this book is to guide you on your journey, help you remember who you truly are, and give you the tools to:

◇ Find the light within you and let go of past issues and hurts.
◇ Uplift and expand your energies.
◇ Help you move faster through challenges.
◇ Return to balance again on all levels of mind, body and spirit.
◇ Find inner peace and happiness.
◇ Reach enlightenment in this lifetime.

CREATING HEAVEN ON EARTH

Our journey to enlightenment involves creating Heaven on Earth, a world you would like to live in. Together we can make this happen. We can create a world where:

◇ Everyone is happy and fulfilled.
◇ There is plenty for everyone, and hunger and poverty belong to the past.
◇ Our planet Earth is respected.
◇ Every person and all animals are loved and honoured.

We are living in exciting times. As each of us experiences more love, joy, peace and fulfilment, we create a ripple effect and send waves of light outwards, touching everyone and everything else around us. As everything is interconnected, our waves of love and light generate the possibility of creating Heaven on Earth.

When we are completely harmonious with everyone and our surroundings, we are in touch with oneness, the divine plan, and we live our lives based on unconditional love. We are enlightened beings.

You will be able to take all the steps outlined in this book—nothing is beyond what you are capable of.

My journey to enlightenment

This book was inspired by my own journey back to wholeness.

I often asked myself, 'How can I write a book about enlightenment, when I haven't reached that stage yet myself?'

The answer soon became clear. Writing this book was part of my own journey to inner peace, happiness and enlightenment. As I wrote each section, it was important that I put everything I was writing into practice myself. In fact, the information was given to me in the order I needed for my own growth and transformation. So, step by step, just as you are about to do, I did the work on myself.

It was a wonderful experience—full of joy, a dash of eureka moments, one or two instances of tiredness and doubt, and many more amazingly uplifting times when I felt full of vitality and in the flow of love, in harmony with all of life.

My wish for you is that this book will guide you to all that fills your heart and soul as you take your own golden journey to enlightenment.

How this book came about

This book was born in the West of Ireland, in the Burren—a mystical place where the mountains meet the wild Atlantic Ocean. I often travel to this special place to rest and be renewed. This is where I am most inspired, and feel closer to my soul than anywhere else. There are no distractions other than the beauty all around me, and the whisperings of Mother Nature.

During the summer of 2013, I knew that something new was being birthed. The dawn called me each day to get up and go for a walk in the fresh clear morning air. My route took me along an ancient green pathway, tucked into the side of a nearby mountain. After about two miles, I left the pathway and carefully descended the craggy and heathery slope to my personal piece of Heaven, my special paradise, where my soul could take a deep breath and expand.

No one above could see that a human being was perched far below, in an armchair which Mother Nature invited me to sit in, formed on her grassy and heathery slope. As I tucked myself in, the heather formed a green and purple blanket all around me, keeping me cosy and dry.

Below me all I could see was the Atlantic Ocean, often alive with gales and white horses dancing on the waves. Pools of light formed on the water as the dawn sent its sparkling rays through the soft morning clouds. Sometimes pods of dolphins came by close to the shore, sending up misty puffs of air. These were truly amazing and magical experiences for me.

The only sounds I could hear were the rolling thunderous waves and the whoosh of the breeze as it tossed through the heather.

It was here, in the total privacy of my writing studio in this peaceful haven, pen and paper in hand as I meditated on the beauty all around me, I was inspired to write this book, guided by many Angels and wise beings from the realms of light.

This was a beautiful meeting place where I could easily connect with the Angels, Saints, Ascended Masters and my Guides, and tap into the higher aspects of my mind and my Higher Self, where wisdom and inspiration flow easily. I invited the Angels to guide and inspire me with words and wisdom infused with divine love, which would touch the hearts of others and assist them on their journey to find inner peace, happiness and enlightenment.

I feel truly blessed and privileged to have received this information, and now I share it with you.

Enlightenment

You can reach enlightenment in this lifetime!

On your journey to enlightenment, you begin to recognise who you truly are: a magnificent being, radiant with love, light, joy and vitality. You can answer the call of your soul to come back to wholeness again.

Enlightenment is a process of expanding your consciousness to such a level that you are aligned with the divine plan. You understand your oneness with everyone and all of creation, and weave peace and harmony all around you.

THERE ARE MANY LEVELS OF ENLIGHTENMENT

People often think that only great beings, such as the Dalai Lama, Buddha, or the many Christian Saints we are familiar with, can reach enlightenment. However, there are many levels of enlightenment, and this book focuses on the levels you can achieve in this lifetime.

WHAT LEVEL OF ENLIGHTENMENT CAN YOU ACHIEVE?

When you are full of love and joy, focused on peaceful and harmonious thoughts, wishing the best for everyone and everything—you are in an enlightened state. At this level, you effortlessly flow into high states of consciousness, where your heart is wide open, and you feel connected to everyone and everything. You see the world as a beautiful place to live, and have no need to judge others as you understand that all of life's events serve your soul's growth.

Your journey to enlightenment is a step-by-step choice. You can choose the most appropriate golden steps for you that will take you to your destination.

Although everyone on Earth is on a journey of spiritual growth, you have your own unique pathway to follow. As you take this journey, your life will start to flow smoother. You will find that situations will calmly fall into place, and you will view all challenges from a higher perspective. You will become lighter, happier and in touch with all the good of life. To reach this level, it is important to let go of old patterns and thoughts that no longer serve you, leaving more time and space for nourishing your mind, body and spirit with enlightened thoughts, actions, and ways of being.

It is important to realise that you have the power within you to transform your life, raise your awareness, and clear out old issues. You can connect with your inner light and potential, where there is love, peace, harmony, joy and vitality.

You can reach enlightenment in this lifetime.

ENLIGHTENED MOMENTS

On your journey to enlightenment, you will have many enlightened moments. What are these moments and how do you recognise them? Well, have you experienced times when you felt radiant with love and happiness, in harmony with everyone and everything? Have you ever felt engulfed with the sensation that all your dreams could actually come true? These are all experiences of expansion and enlightenment.

Remember your experiences of enlightenment and build on them.

HIGHER LEVELS OF ENLIGHTENMENT

As you take each golden step on your journey, you start to experience pure consciousness and become one with your Higher Self, the most loving and wise aspect of who you are. At this level you can instantly create and manifest. Your consciousness can touch the consciousness within all matter, that matter which is formed and formless. You experience true oneness, and help others create Heaven here on Earth.

At even higher levels, you realise there is much work to be done in other dimensions within the cosmos. You can become an initiate in the spiritual realms and assist many enlightened beings. You may work with many Angels, Guides, Saints and Ascended Masters, to carry out divine tasks to spread love and harmony throughout all the realms of creation, and assist many others to reach enlightenment.

ASSISTANCE FROM THE SPIRITUAL REALMS

There is a constant source of divine love, and many great beings of light in the spiritual realms, Angels, Guides, Saints and Ascended Masters, that you can call upon at any time for guidance and inspiration. The light and wisdom of your Higher Self and soul is also available to you at all times.

NEW GOLDEN AGE OF ENLIGHTENMENT

Our world is in transition right now as we move from the world we have known for a very long time, to a bright new golden world where we will live as enlightened beings of love and peace, creating harmonious frequencies and events all around us.

This time of transformation is heralding a new beginning and way of being, and you have an important role to play. Each person's contribution is important, and together we can create a beautiful world to live in.

You have choices and opportunities like never before to raise your consciousness and levels of light, to find inner peace and happiness, and reach enlightenment in this lifetime.

A word of encouragement as you start on this journey

How would you feel if you knew that the essence of who you are, the light of your soul, is that of infinite love and light, and that you are already an enlightened being?

Take a few moments to acknowledge the magnificence of who you are — this is the most empowering thought you can have.

Know that you already have an abundance of love, light, joy, peace, harmony and contentment within you — all the qualities of enlightenment.

I invite you to take a few moments to let this powerful statement sink in, as our vision of who we truly are can sometimes become clouded by the concerns and challenges of day-to-day living.

It is empowering to know that all the qualities of enlightenment can be strengthened. As you explore this book, you will be given guidance and many tools to work with, which will bring you back to the truth of who you are. Sometimes it takes just a moment of awareness — a moment of positive thinking — to awaken and remember who you are, and accept the great gift of enlightenment and freedom which it brings.

YOU ARE AN ENLIGHTENED BEING — YOUR ESSENCE IS DIVINE

To start you on your journey, I want to show you a few simple steps you can take which can help you become aware of your divine essence.

STEPS FOR CONNECTING WITH YOUR DIVINE ESSENCE

1. Take a few moments to get comfortable and relaxed. You might like to play soft and gentle music in the background.

2. Bring your attention to your heart area. This is your centre for giving and receiving love. Become aware of the love within your heart. You might find it helpful to hold thoughts in your mind of a person, child, or pet you love unconditionally. Or, bring to mind a time you felt held and loved, and become aware of the love in your heart expanding.

3. Remember a time when you felt great joy. Let the feeling of joy bubble up within your heart, and allow its exuberant energy envelop you.

4. Focus on a time when you felt at peace with yourself and the world. Connect with the calmness that comes from knowing that all is well.

5. Let this peaceful inner feeling expand, until you start to flow with feelings of harmony.

6. Allow yourself some time to experience the contentment of your soul, which is now radiant with love, joy, peace and harmony.

Spend a few moments relaxing and bathing in these wonderful energies — your own divine essence.

 Know that you are special beyond words.

It takes just a few moments to do this exercise but in it you can experience amazing transformation. Know that by doing the exercise you are laying the foundation stone for your journey to enlightenment.

As you shine your light, you create a radiant ripple, like a pebble dropped in a lake, sending waves of love and light out to touch everyone and everything around you. You will become a beacon for others, bringing the possibility of creating Heaven on Earth.

How to use this book

To get the most benefit from this book, I suggest that you read it once in its entirety. When you have finished, you can return to the chapters which are most relevant to you at that moment and concentrate on them. Spend some time working with those chapters, and then focus on the next sections you are drawn to. Working this way will lead you gently, but powerfully, along your own golden pathway to inner peace, happiness, and enlightenment.

Please take your time as you make your way through the book, and review your progress regularly.

Notice:
◊   How you feel.
◊   How other people react to you.
◊   The transformations taking place in your life.

You will find you will reach a deeper level of clarity, wisdom and understanding about your life and how to live well.

There are great truths and simplicities in this book. Allow them to speak to your heart. Always follow your inner guidance and do what is right for you. Allow this book and your own innate wisdom to guide you.

As you embark on your journey with this book, be prepared to move from the mundane into the light of infinite possibilities. Sometimes it takes only a reminder of what's possible for you to reach for the transformation and infinite possibilities life has to offer.

FIVE MEDITATIONS

As you read the book, you may find it helpful to listen to the five free MP3 recordings which relate to various sections within the book.

1. Fifteen minute relaxation — to refresh your mind, body and spirit.
2. Merge with your Higher Self — the light of your soul.
3. Golden Angelic Cloak of Light.
4. Oval of Heavenly Light — an experience of enlightenment.
5. DNA Healing — cleanse and reprogramme your DNA with new life and energy.

Full details are on page vi.

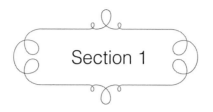

Section 1

Love and joy are the keys to enlightenment

Live with love and joy in your heart, two of the most important qualities to foster as you take your golden steps towards inner peace, happiness and enlightenment.

Each of the golden steps you take will be based on love and joy. Therefore, this first section will give detailed guidelines on how to increase the flow of love and joy in your life.

Love

 Within your heart resides a divine spark, the loving essence of who you are.

There is a flow of love within our universe. It is the fabric which binds everything together, right down to the smallest particles in existence. We spend our lives exploring the many facets of love as we answer the call of our soul to return to love and become whole again.

 Love and all its many reflections — compassion, empathy, acceptance, peace, kindness, harmony and forgiveness — are the keys to enlightenment.

ENCOURAGING LOVE TO BLOSSOM

Love is our natural state of being. It is the key to empathy and understanding, which ultimately dissolves barriers and enhances relationships. Love blossoms when we open our hearts and act with harmlessness towards all, knowing each person is part of the magnificent tapestry of life.

We are all on our unique journey, with many things to learn and experience during our lifetime. We all like to be validated, so it is easier to be around people who agree with us. However, we live in a world of many differing opinions. We encourage love to flourish when we support each other, accept our different choices, values and priorities, and let go of the need to be right.

Let us be kind to each other, because we do not know how everyone else is feeling deep inside.

I think that most of us, myself included, would like to be able to look back at the end of our lives and be able to say that we did our best to extend love to others, regardless of their circumstance or how they were behaving.

You energise the divine flow of love and call it into your life and the lives of others simply through your willingness to love.

> Spread love wherever you go. Let no one ever come to you without leaving happier.
> —Mother Teresa

LOVE HEALS

Love is at the heart of every religion. It is the greatest healer, and transforms all. Nothing negative can exist in the presence of love. When offered in its purest form, all barriers dissolve, and bridges are built.

 One person extending the hand of love is the link in the chain, offering a connection to others.

Love dissolves hurt and pain on all levels, both physical and emotional. You may have witnessed a child who has fallen over and grazed its knee being soothed by a loving mother, whose tender kiss on the sore spot takes away the pain. You can do the same for yourself by placing a gentle and loving hand on a sore spot, and witness the pain miraculously disappear, or healing taking place. This is true for all types of healing. It is the flow of divine love channelled through a healer's hands which heals and renews.

BEING IN LOVE

As we connect soul to soul with another, we experience both a sense of expansion and oneness. Our soul longs for this experience of union, helping us remember who we truly are—great beings of light present in this physical world, learning, growing, and returning to an enlightened state of being.

Our friendships and relationships provide us with mirrors, enabling us to see aspects of ourselves that are hidden from view. We may be stretched in many ways, which is why it is important to cultivate loving connections with others so we can embrace our growth and life's lessons, all the while held safely in the arms of love.

> Love is a gift of one's innermost soul to another so both can be whole.
> —Gautama Buddha

UNCONDITIONAL LOVE

Many people ask, 'What is unconditional love?' The answer is simple; it is pure love, given without any conditions or hopes of receiving something in return. Unconditional love comes from our purest state of consciousness because this is the essence of who we are—great beings of light and love.

We don't form cords or attachments to anyone when we love unconditionally as we don't have any expectations of them, only a desire to grace them with love.

STEPS FOR OFFERING UNCONDITIONAL LOVE

1. Take your focus within to the pure, divine spark of love within your heart. Imagine beams of love travelling from your heart to anyone you know who is in need of a little extra love, or to

anyone who has hurt you. Do this, not to change them, but to offer love, acceptance and forgiveness, with no strings attached.

2.   As you bring each person to mind, sending a beam of unconditional love, there may be a word or message you also want to send, for instance:
I offer you …
   ◇   Love and acceptance.
   ◇   Forgiveness and peace.
   ◇   Happiness and abundance.
   ◇   Fulfilment of all your hopes and dreams.
   ◇   Health and vitality.

3.   Although your love is unconditional, asking for nothing in return, rest for a moment and notice how your heart is now overflowing with love.

There is a divine flow of love throughout the Universe. Love always responds to love, being awakened or returned through the simple act of loving.

OPENING YOUR HEART TO LOVE

We are brought into this world with open hearts full of love and joy. However, as we go through life with its many experiences—sometimes hurtful and fearful—we start to put up barriers to protect ourselves. We also put up barriers to cage in emotions and the parts of ourselves we don't want others to see.

These barriers come in the form of the personality traits we develop to protect ourselves. They are like armour, keeping others out and blocking love coming in, while also closing our hearts off to giving love. Our energy no longer flows freely, and we can become stuck, cut off from the love we so desire to give and receive.

You can remove the barriers to love and return again to a glorious state of radiant love.

STEPS TO OPENING YOUR HEART AND TAKING DOWN THE ARMOUR

1. First of all, place your hands over your heart, and bring to mind someone you love unconditionally; for instance, a child, pet or partner. You will become aware of a warm glow of love forming in the centre of your chest.

2. Imagine your heart's centre opening gently, like the petals of a rose at the dawn of the day. Know that your own heart is like a beautiful rose, each petal representing all the love you are capable of giving, with a golden centre of unlimited potential.

3. Let this golden centre of light shine on the rose petals of your heart, transforming stagnant and old energies to love, dissolving hurt and grief.

4. Ask yourself, 'Am I ready to take down my armour and set myself free?'

   You might also like to ask:
   ◇ Why did I need this armour or protection?
   ◇ Is it time to break down the armour?

5. Imagine removing the armour, layer by layer. What do the layers look like? Perhaps like barbed wire, building blocks, or a screen you can hide behind?

6. As the layers are removed, see old hurts, insecurities and fears, anger, behaviours, all things hiding behind your armour, being transformed by the golden light, leaving you *fresh, free* and *light*.

7.   Look at yourself with your heart wide open, and see that there isn't anything to be afraid of. Accept that you no longer need armour to keep anything out, or in.

8.   Rest for a few moments while focusing on your radiant heart centre, now shining with rays of love and light, reaching out and touching everyone and everything around you, gifting them with love.

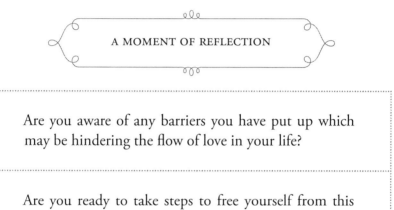

A MOMENT OF REFLECTION

Are you aware of any barriers you have put up which may be hindering the flow of love in your life?

Are you ready to take steps to free yourself from this restriction?

OPEN YOUR HEART AND BUILD BRIDGES

It is easier to love those who love us in return. However, whenever we find someone difficult or challenging, love asks us to open our hearts and spread its tender grace of love and kindness, which ultimately dissolves barriers and builds bridges.

STEPS FOR BUILDING BRIDGES

1.   Think of a person you find difficult or challenging. Take your focus within, to your centre of pure love, and ask your Higher Self—the most loving and wise aspect of who you are—to

help you deal with this person in the most loving way possible. Ask for the highest truths about your relationship with this person, and for the situation you find yourself in to be revealed to you. As you hold this thought, you are in touch with the higher workings of your mind and heart.

2.   Let the feeling of love within your heart bubble up and intensify, so you can almost see rays of love, of every colour imaginable, radiating out from your heart.

3.   Imagine a rainbow bridge of light forming between yourself and the other person. The rainbow's colours represent all the qualities of love—compassion, acceptance, empathy, gentleness, forgiveness—and a wish of happiness for the other person, that they may receive all their heart's desires.

4.   Put aside any tensions or concerns about what has happened between both of you. Know that the situation can be transformed by love.

5.   Imagine walking over the bridge to meet the other person. You approach them with love in your heart.

6.   Does the other person start to walk across the bridge to meet you halfway? We can't control how others feel or respond, but we can plant the seeds of love which heal and transform.

7.   Whatever their decision, you know that your heart is open and that the bridge will remain so that they can meet you when the time is right.

RECIPE FOR STAYING IN LOVE

Do whatever you can to stay in love with yourself and others.

Within a recipe for staying in love, as in all recipes, there are many ingredients to choose from, depending on your taste and needs. The following are a few guidelines to help keep the doorway to the flow of love open.

◇ Be kind and gentle with yourself—send love and acceptance to all parts of you. You will uncover the jewel at the centre of your being, all that you already are—a divine, loving, radiant and beautiful soul.

◇ See love wherever you go—in every person, place, and situation.

◇ Be kind to others and ask, 'What is the most loving way for me to handle this situation, person or challenge?'

◇ Aim to see the best in everyone, even if sometimes you have to look a little deeper to find their light. Know that it is there.

◇ Bless everyone with love and compassion. Know that they have many challenges and make mistakes just as you do. They are human. There will be many times when you aren't aware of the challenges and difficulties others are facing.

◇ See love in every situation, even if it isn't apparent there and then. Love is always present and just by perceiving it, you energise it, and call it forward.

◇ Be grateful for everything, even the simple things in life. Gratitude will open your heart.

◇ Stay focused in the present moment, where miracles are possible.

◇ Make sure that you pencil in time for self-love and nurturing. For instance, have a luxurious bath with soft music and candlelight, or go for a walk in nature. Do lots of joyful things—have fun, play, rest and enjoy life.

Share the gift of your love. Remember who you are — a radiant being of light and love.

Unconditional love flows from your purest state of consciousness. You create a beautiful and enlightened world as you send a stream of love from your heart to touch everyone and everything around you.

Living joyfully

 Every moment is an opportunity to invite even more joy into your life.

We are moving into a bright new era, where we will have new opportunities to live lives full of happiness, harmony and balance. While we may be presented with many lessons to support our growth and evolution, ultimately our journey to wholeness starts with living joyfully.

How do you feel when you are full of joy? Being joyful lightens your energies, and is essential on the journey to enlightenment. Don't forget that the word 'light' is the core of 'enlightenment'.

HEAL THE PAST AND LIVE JOYFULLY

Have you ever watched a toddler playing? A child doesn't have those hurts and issues that build up over many years, and therefore radiates a natural state of happiness. It is important that we heal and let go of the hurts and past issues dragging us down, so we are free to express our natural state of happiness. (A later chapter on Tools for Transformation offers guidance on how to heal and release old burdens.)

Joy is an attractive quality, and under the Law of Attraction it brings many more opportunities for happiness, and for wonderful people, things and events to come into our lives.

BEING JOYFUL IN THE PRESENT MOMENT

Sometimes you may be in a great flow of happiness and it feels good. But no matter what you may be doing, every moment offers an opportunity to be joyful. For instance, if you are cooking, you can stay mindful in the experience. Watch your thoughts and focus on doing the task with love. Not only will you feel brighter and happier, but your food will be infused with love, and people may even comment that the flavours are enhanced!

The same applies to everything you do during the day. Stay centred, mindful in the experience, and think happy thoughts. Watch as the joy is returned to you tenfold.

YOUR LIFE CAN BE A JOYFUL EXPERIENCE

Doing whatever you find joyous and fulfilling accelerates your journey to enlightenment.

When I hold spiritual classes on *Finding Your Soul Purpose*, I lead people in exercises to help them focus internally and connect with their inner wisdom. The first exercise we always start with is to look at what brings us the most joy in life. I ask people to make a list of ten things they love to do, and the atmosphere becomes electric and supercharged with happy vibes.

We all have unique gifts and talents to share with others, and we create a beautiful world when we are happy and fulfilled. This includes doing jobs that we enjoy, and activities and hobbies which nurture us.

YOUR LIFE PURPOSE

Many people today are asking, 'What is my life purpose?' I believe that our collective purpose is to nurture the growth of our souls, realise who we are (self-realisation or enlightenment) and live loving, joyful lives in harmony with each other.

Whatever nurtures your heart and soul is closely aligned with your own individual life purpose. Heart-opening and joyful experiences are signals from your soul that you are on the right path.

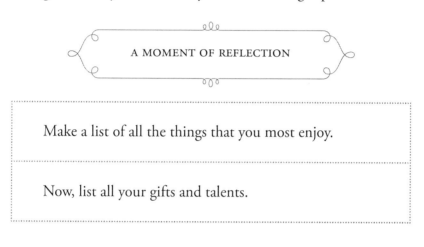

A MOMENT OF REFLECTION

Make a list of all the things that you most enjoy.

Now, list all your gifts and talents.

FINDING JOY IN THE WORK YOU DO

Finding a job where you are able to offer your gifts and talents, while doing something you really enjoy, is ideal. If you are not doing the job you would love, are there any steps that you can take to explore other positions, or to retrain?

Remember to always be joyful in the present moment. Even if you do not decide to look for another job, you can still find joy in what you are doing by appreciating the benefits of your present position, watching your thoughts, and doing each task with love. Try to look forward to the new ventures you are planning. Your light and happy heart will attract new opportunities into your life.

MY STORY: FOLLOWING THE CALLING OF MY SOUL

I worked as an administrative assistant in a large government department for twenty-one years. While I enjoyed the job and the great relationships I had with friends and colleagues, I started to feel an overwhelming desire to leave. There were many reasons to stay; it gave great job security, and I had a mortgage. However, the desire to leave and move on was so strong that I had to take action.

With a little planning and saving, I took a six-month sabbatical, and made a list of all the things I wanted to do during this special time. As I had spent so much time in an office, I particularly wanted to spend time outdoors. Incredibly, I was offered two jobs straight away—one as a hostel warden, the other as a mountain leader in an outdoor centre.

So, I set off on a new adventure.

As it turned out, I only worked for the first six weeks, as there were so many things left on my list that I wanted to do, and I was enjoying the taste of freedom. This 'time out' was essential for me, as during a quiet time walking in the forest, I received a very clear message from my Higher Self that a new phase of my life was about to begin. It was time to start making plans.

I went back to work cheerfully after my six months away, and started to retrain as an aromatherapist and healer in preparation for a new career, following the calling of my soul.

LETTING GO AND MOVING ON

 When you let go of something, you create a space for something new to take its place. Focus on the golden opportunities that are coming your way.

There are many different phases in our lives, and our inner guidance often calls us to let go and move on. We step into our power when we realise we can follow the guidance of our heart and soul, and let go with love.

It can take a lot of courage to give up something or go in a new direction, especially when it involves stepping into the unknown. There are many reasons why we may hesitate. Our lack of action or indecision is usually based on:

◇ Fear of change.
◇ Fear of letting people down.
◇ Fear of what people will say.
◇ Worries about whether the new plan will work out.
◇ Feeling responsible and worried that if we don't do what is required, everything will fall apart.

WHAT IS STOPPING YOU?

It is helpful to make your own list of what is stopping you from changing, from letting go or moving on. Deal with all the worries, thoughts, and practical issues involved.

Ask yourself some important questions relevant to the changes you are contemplating, such as:

◇ What will I miss out on if I don't move forward?
◇ Is it time for someone else to do this task and have this experience?
◇ What will happen if I continue in the same role or doing the same thing?

CHANGE: STEP-BY-STEP PLANNING

For most people, change is a step-by-step process, which often requires planning. Planning involves taking responsibility for your life and shows spiritual maturity, so it is best to take the time to do it.

Your plan may involve retraining, part-time work, delegating responsibility to others, ending a relationship, or freeing up some time. Whatever change you are aiming for, plan well, and examine all the steps you need to take to reach your goal.

You deserve the life of your dreams. You can make it happen.

FREEDOM TO LIVE JOYFULLY

You are born to experience joy and to share happiness with others.

Do you find in your busy life that there often isn't enough time to get through everything you have to do? Most of us set our priorities around work or household tasks, all of which need to be tended to. However, it is also important to set some time aside for ourselves, to nurture our body, mind and soul.

I invite you to do the next exercise and follow the two steps below. This will give focus to activities which nourish you and bring you the greatest joy. The simple pleasures in life are often the most rewarding.

STEPS FOR MAKING TIME FOR FUN AND JOY IN YOUR LIFE

STEP 1: Make a list of three things you are going to do to pamper and nurture yourself over the next few weeks. It is best to keep it simple, for instance, having a warm bath with soft music and candlelight, setting aside time to read your book, going on a family day out, or a quiet walk in a beautiful place in nature. You may find it helpful to plan to do some activities by yourself, so you aren't trying to fit into someone else's schedule.

STEP 2: Write down a time and date for this joyful activity. This is important, as when you mark it in your diary or calendar, it becomes a definite date.

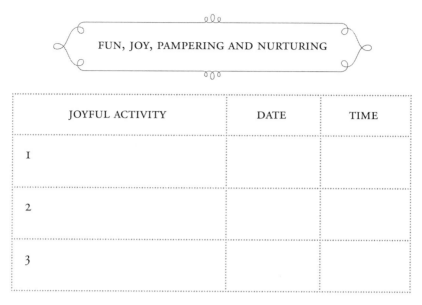

	JOYFUL ACTIVITY	DATE	TIME
I			
2			
3			

FINDING TIME TO DO THE THINGS YOU ENJOY

You may find that, with so much happening in your life, there isn't enough time to do the things you most enjoy. If so, I invite you to create a Balance and Harmony Chart, similar to the one shown below. This will help you clearly see how you are spending your time, pinpoint areas that you can change, or to set new priorities if you need to.

JOYFUL LIVING — BALANCE AND HARMONY

The chart below is an example of how one person spends a typical day.

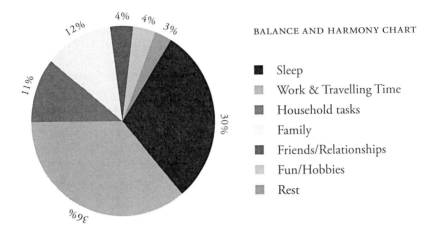

Most people find that the time spent on fun or relationships can be quite small, while the section allocated to work takes up most of the day.

YOUR BALANCE AND HARMONY CHART

Draw your own chart, using headings that are most relevant to how you spend your day. Review your chart, and take note of the parts you are happy with and those you would like to change.

Now that you can see exactly how you are spending your time, have you found any areas you want to change, enabling you to free up more time for yourself and other activities?

SIMPLE WAYS TO BRING LIGHT AND SPARKLE TO YOUR DAY

Life is not measured by the number of breaths we take,
but by the moments that take our breath away.
—Author unknown

There are many ways to add more light and sparkle to your day. I have outlined a couple of short exercises below which you can try.

BREATHE IN LIGHTNESS AND JOY

1. Spend a few moments focusing on the joyful qualities you would like in your life today; for instance, love, laughter, beauty, and vitality.

2. As you breathe in, draw each of these qualities inside and bathe every cell of your body with their radiance.

3. Rest for a few minutes, and enjoy the good feelings.

FOCUS ON HAPPY THOUGHTS

◇ You can uplift and change your thoughts by focusing for a few minutes on the wonder of life—its sparkle, specialness and gifts. For instance, you may like to think of your child's smile, your pet's loving greeting, the gifts of nature, your cosy home, the memory of marvellous times, or anticipation of future events.
◇ You can choose to hold happy thoughts. Reach for the sparkle and let your spirit soar.

BE JOYFUL AND FOLLOW YOUR HEART'S DESIRE

Your heart is the joyful centre of your being, the giver and receiver of love, and the nurturing essence of life. It is important to follow the guidance of your heart.

Take time to nurture your heart's desire as often as you can, as this will keep you on your life's path, opening you to joy and fulfilment effortlessly.

  You deserve to have your heart's desire fulfilled.

MAKE THE MOST OF LIFE

We often hear the phrase *'live each day as if it is your last'*. There is great wisdom in these words. The time to live life to the full is right now. Why put off until tomorrow that which could bring you all the fulfilment and richness of life today?

Now is the moment to:
◇   Appreciate all the wonderful people in your life.
◇   Plan a new adventure.
◇   Enrol in a new class.
◇   Start a new project.
◇   Take a walk in nature.
◇   Smile and enjoy life.

Every moment is an opportunity to live joyfully. Appreciate all you have in your life, and all the fresh opportunities you can create.

SMILING HELPS US FEEL MORE ALIVE AND JOYFUL

Have you noticed that when you see someone smile, you often just can't help but smile too? It's contagious. In fact, the image of a smiling person activates a part of our brain which controls the movements of our face, and we automatically form a grin. We can trigger our joyful smile simply by holding happy thoughts, or memories of some of the best moments in our lives.

Nobody teaches a baby how to smile. It is part of their own natural exuberance which simply bubbles up. It is a joy to be around smiling babies, as they remind us of our own innocence and innate happiness. Smiling is an inherent part of our essence, and is a way of showing others the light and joy of our soul. It also sends comforting messages to let people know that we appreciate and see the best in them.

LET YOUR SMILE BRING JOY TO THE WORLD

I invite you to contribute to the well-being of this planet by letting your smile shine out and uplift everyone around you. Your smile can be a beacon of love and joy to brighten up the world.

Smile, and the whole world smiles with you.

TREAT LIFE AS AN ADVENTURE

Take a leap into the swirling adventure of life and open yourself to the excitement, sparkle and joy of each new day.

1.   Ask yourself—what will bring you the most joy and satisfaction today?

2.   Can you add even more adventure to your day? Is there something new you would like to try, or approach something in a different way? The possibilities are limitless.

Repeat the following words often.

Life is wonderful!

Let them inspire and energise you, and keep you in touch with your joyful and youthful nature.

Pause and review

Take a breath and pause for a moment. Spend a few minutes reviewing your experience of the various exercises in this section.

 What exercises did you particularly enjoy?

 Make a note of the wise thoughts or insights you received.

 Have you pinpointed areas where you can increase the love and joy in your life?

How do you think your life would be if you put the things you have learned so far into regular practice?

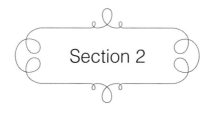

Section 2

Light up your life

We have all felt tired and drained, worries etched into our faces, the weight of the world on our shoulders. However, when you release these burdens and light up your life with happiness, love and peace, you will glow with youthful energy.

This section will help you light up your life, create golden opportunities, and clear your pathway to enlightenment.

Blessings

Send blessings and invite divine grace and miracles into your life.

Blessings confer a divine grace — a healing energy — which lifts everyone and everything to higher levels of love and light, ensuring the best possible outcome in all situations.

In a world where our thoughts, words and actions have a creative energy, the divine grace offered by blessings dissolves lower thoughts and emotions, and miracles can happen. When you send blessings, your heart opens to soften every situation with love, compassion and forgiveness, making them easier to resolve.

SENDING BLESSINGS TO PEOPLE AND SITUATIONS

It is very powerful to send blessings to anyone who has not treated you the way you would have liked. You can choose to send blessings, wish them all the joy, love and success they desire, and visualise them smiling and happy. Just as you sometimes feel vulnerable, know that they too are vulnerable and are doing what they can, to the best of their knowledge.

It is an amazing and uplifting experience to send blessings to all irritating situations, large and small. Irritation and anger are strong, reactive emotions. Your mind can be consumed with thoughts of what you would like to say or do. However, you can decide to pause for a moment before reacting. This is a special moment, and in this moment you can invoke divine grace and send blessings to heal and transform.

EXAMPLES OF BLESSINGS

Bless the person or situation with a divine quality, or with the perfect outcome for them. Imagine the situation is already transformed and perfected.

If someone has hurt you, think or say:
'I bless you with love.'

If someone has been cruel, think or say:
'I bless you with compassion.'

If someone has taken something belonging to you, think or say:
'I bless you with abundance.'

If someone has been impatient, think or say:
'I bless you with patience.'

If someone has been angry with you, think or say:
'I bless you with peace and all your heart desires.'

For countries at war, think or say:
'I bless these countries [name them] and their people with peace.'

For complex situations, think or say:
'I bless [name the person(s)] and this situation [name the situation] with a perfect solution that will enhance everyone's life.'

People often ask how many times they should send blessings. You may only need to send the blessing once. For a more challenging situation, or where there are strong emotions, send blessings as often as you remember during the day, perhaps for several days. Also, focus on the outcome being for the highest good of all.

TRANSFORMATION THROUGH BLESSINGS

As you send blessings to others, you also receive the divine grace offered by the blessing. This higher frequency transforms your thoughts and emotions so that you light up with the highest potential and possibilities.

MAURA'S STORY

Maura worked in a busy office, and although she was often under pressure, she worked diligently to get through her workload. She always did the best she could, and felt that she was doing her job really well.

As such, she was very surprised when she received a curt email from a colleague criticising the progress she was making on a project they were both working on. Maura felt hurt, unappreciated and angry. She wondered if her colleagues knew about the complaint, and naturally her mind started to fill up with thoughts about how best to defend herself.

Over the next few days Maura could hardly do any work as she was so angry and depressed. Another colleague at work noticed that she was looking very tired and sad, and they spoke about what had happened. The colleague advised Maura that it was time to stop letting this one complaint take over her life, and she told her about the healing power of blessings.

On hearing this, Maura felt like a light had been switched on and decided to give it a go. She sent blessings to her colleague, wishing him happiness and success in all areas of his life, and particularly in the work he was doing (including their joint project).

As she was very hurt, Maura continued to send blessings for a few days. Her anger and depression started to fade and to her surprise, she found herself writing a very polite email to her colleague asking if he would like to meet with her to discuss his concerns and see if they could get back on track.

When they met, he was understanding and supportive, and very open to hearing her point of view. He apologised for sending the first email, and explained he had sent it in a moment of anger as he had been feeling under a lot of pressure.

In this case, sending blessings allowed a divine grace to flow to all involved and brought forgiveness, understanding and lightness to the situation. Thanks to this, Maura and her colleague could work in harmony again.

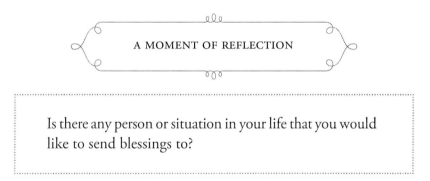

A MOMENT OF REFLECTION

Is there any person or situation in your life that you would like to send blessings to?

Appreciation

Appreciation opens your heart and allows you to soar with all the good in life, opening doorways to higher levels of love, light, peace and joy.

Appreciation uplifts your soul and is one of the keys to enlightenment. It soothes conflict, and creates opportunities for greater understanding and enhanced relationships.

Appreciation asks you to suspend judgement and misunderstandings, and focus instead on the goodness, light and radiance within yourself and others. Every situation can be softened or turned around by appreciation. It adds a little sparkle of light to your life, transforming disappointment and hurt to positivity. Above all, it opens your heart and helps you create a life based on happiness and joy.

CREATING A WORLD WHERE WE CAN ALL THRIVE

Each person is a unique soul, with a divine mission to fulfil during their lifetime. Because of our individuality, we live in a world of many differing opinions and realities. As we appreciate and accept each other, we enter into a flow of love and light, goodness and harmony, which uplifts every situation and helps us create a world where we can all thrive and fulfil our soul's mission.

When you send appreciation, you give attention and focus to what is good in your life and the lives of others. You energise the positive, allowing even more good to come to you.

However, the opposite is also true. If your focus is on what has gone wrong, or if you are critical of others, you energise the negative and stay at that level. You shape your reality with your thoughts, words and actions.

Appreciation allows you take a golden step upwards to a new level — a higher frequency of love, understanding and joy — uplifting each person and situation, making miracles possible.

EXAMPLES OF POSITIVE STATEMENTS OF APPRECIATION

> Even though we didn't see eye to eye on this, I appreciate all you have done for me and thank you for your kindness.

> I didn't get the job I wanted, but I appreciate the experience I had in going for the interview and I'm ready to put myself forward for the next position.

> I'm disappointed my holiday is cancelled but I appreciate the extra time I now have to catch up with friends and do all the things I haven't had time to do.

> I'm upset that things didn't go the way I wanted them to, but I appreciate all I have learned from this situation.

STEPS FOR DISSOLVING CONFLICT AND NEGATIVITY

1. Bring to mind a relationship or situation that you feel sad, worried, anxious or angry about.

2. Focus on what you appreciate about the person or situation. For example, their uniqueness, talents, compassion, generosity, and loving nature. Alternatively, you can focus on the gift offered by the challenging situation itself.

3. Imagine speaking to the person, or discussing the situation, as if you were speaking from your Higher Self, the wisest aspect of who you are. Invite your Higher Self to open you to a new understanding and perspective, where you know the most loving words to use, or action to take, so you can resolve the situation.

4. Notice your heart opening as tension, anger or anxiety dissipates, and understanding and gentleness can now enter.

5. Now that you are aligned with the highest way of resolving the situation, you can take whatever positive action is appropriate when the time is right.

APPRECIATING YOURSELF

Sometimes the person we need to appreciate the most is ourselves. While it is nice to receive acknowledgement and appreciation from others, you don't need to wait for this to happen. Appreciating yourself, exactly as you are, uplifts your spirit and makes you stronger. It also makes it easier to appreciate others, as what you give to yourself, you can give to others.

SIMPLE EXERCISE IN SELF-APPRECIATION

1. Write a letter to yourself, acknowledging all the qualities you appreciate about the amazing person that you are; for instance, your loving and understanding nature, your gifts and talents, your body, etc. If you like, you can imagine that your wise and strong inner persona is writing the letter. Let your pen flow as if it has a life of its own, uncensored and excited for this opportunity to tell you all it loves about you.

2. It is good fun to post the letter to yourself, or ask a friend to post it to you after a few weeks.

Gratitude

 Gratitude opens your heart and attracts even more love and joy into your life.

Expressing thanks is a quality of enlightenment which opens your heart and lifts your soul to higher levels of love and joy. Gratitude raises your frequency, cleanses your aura, and puts you into a flow of love which lightens up your life.

GRATITUDE SETS THE LAW OF ATTRACTION IN MOTION

The lightness you feel when you are grateful and open-hearted is an attractive force. Like attracts like, so an open heart attracts even more love, abundance and joyful events into your life. All that you are grateful for will increase.

◇ When you give thanks for the amount you earn, you draw even more abundance to you.
◇ When you give thanks for your good health, your body responds and radiates health and vitality.
◇ Being grateful for the friendships in your life attracts more wonderful people to you.
◇ Being thankful for all you have in your life opens doorways for more to come in.

MY STORY: BEING THANKFUL FOR GOOD HEALTH

One day I had a mild headache, and was completely focused on the pain and inconvenience it was causing. It was like having a carpet with a tiny stain and only being able to see that small flaw, rather than the full, magnificent carpet.

Then I remembered that the rest of my body was functioning really well, and I thanked my body for being so vibrant and healthy. My body responded to the new lightness I felt, and my headache eased, then disappeared.

You can choose to give thanks for all you have, in every area of your life, and even more will come to you.

GRATITUDE AND CHOICES

Whatever your challenges in life, there is always something to be thankful for. Gratitude will elevate you to a higher frequency and a flow of love, soothing anxieties and worries, and helping you see things from a higher perspective.

As a human being, you have been given the gift of choice. Giving thanks for the gift of your life, for the choices you can make and the decisions you can take, allows even more new directions and wonderful experiences to unfold.

GRATITUDE JOURNAL

I highly recommend that you buy a special book with blank pages and keep a gratitude journal. Before you go to sleep at night, write a list of some things you are grateful for; for example, all the wonderful things that happened during the day, work that went well, your friendships, the walk you had in pleasant sunshine, the bus arriving in time, your child's smile — the list is endless.

Follow this up in the morning by starting your day positively. Before getting out of bed, give thanks for all the possibilities of the wonderful day ahead. The brightness of a new day, a lovely breakfast, exciting people you will meet, etc. Fill your mind with thoughts of gratitude and love, and your day will be transformed.

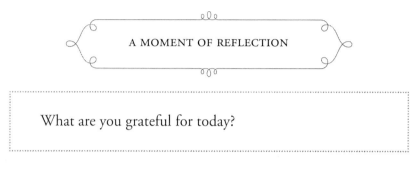

A MOMENT OF REFLECTION

What are you grateful for today?

Developing an 'attitude of gratitude' opens your heart to abundance.

A bright start to your day

 A new day is born each morning, full of light, joy and wonderful possibilities.

MORNING RITUAL TO LIGHTEN UP YOUR DAY

As each new day dawns, you are offered fresh opportunities to create more love, happiness and fulfilment in your life. The morning is a wonderful time to bless and brighten your day.

It can take as little as five minutes to prepare for the day ahead. This is time well spent—you will find that you are clearer, happier and can accomplish more with grace and ease.

Some suggestions for giving yourself a bright start to the day are outlined below. You might like to use these ideas to create your own special blend to nurture your heart and soul.

SUGGESTIONS FOR A FIVE MINUTE MORNING PREPARATION

◇ Start by lighting a candle and dedicating your day to the highest good. This will bring transformation and lightness to everything you see and do.
◇ Give thanks for the perfection of this new day and ask that it be filled with exciting possibilities.
◇ Take a few moments to invite your Higher Self and your Angels to guide and inspire you, and to arrange magical synchronicities and miracles.
◇ You can also ask your Higher Self and Angels to help you with any challenges you anticipate for the day ahead, resolving

everything in the best possible way, for the highest good of all.

◇ Affirm that you will see only love and goodness in every situation and person you meet.

◇ Hold an image in your mind of everything working out perfectly. Take a few moments to focus on how this will change your day, now that you have a new perspective on the challenges you were anticipating.

◇ Flush your mind with radiant white light to clear your mind of any clutter, fears, anger, sadness or anything that may hold you back.

◇ Your thoughts create the energy around you. You can recreate this energy simply by watching what you are thinking, and holding the highest thoughts about everyone and every situation.

◇ Affirm that your day will be filled with happiness, peace and harmony, and any other qualities you want to call into your life.

◇ Bless the day with a special prayer or inspirational words and ask to be guided to do what is for your highest good, and the good of all. (A sample blessing is outlined below.)

Allow your day be transformed and to unfold in a perfect way.

UPLIFTING THOUGHTS AT THE START OF THE DAY

Reading blessings or inspiring words is like a cleansing balm, soothing frayed emotions and enriching your life.

Take your time in reading the following inspirational passage and blessing—let the words speak to your heart and soul.

POSITIVE THOUGHTS FOR THE DAY

Today is a wonderful new day full of light, joy and amazing possibilities. Today I will be all I am capable of being, and spread light, joy and comfort to others.

My day will unfold in a perfect way. I will move gracefully through any challenges, and find the highest solutions, for the highest good of all.

MY MORNING BLESSING

I invite my Guardian Angel to step in close and enfold me in your loving arms. Please open my heart to radiant love and fill me with joy, peace and clarity.

I align myself with the highest aspect of who I am, my Higher Self, and ask that everything I do today be guided by the wisdom and light of my soul.

I offer myself as an Ambassador for the Light, to spread love, peace and blessings to everyone.

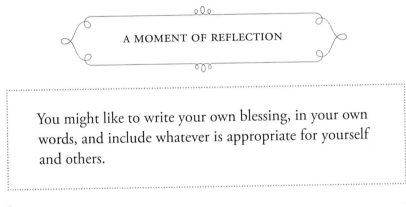

A MOMENT OF REFLECTION

You might like to write your own blessing, in your own words, and include whatever is appropriate for yourself and others.

Bless your day and allow it to unfold in a perfect way.

Look for the gift in challenging situations

 There is a constant flow of love throughout the Universe. When one door closes, another door opens with a golden opportunity.

Sometimes life events don't go the way we would like them to. Nothing remains the same. Life offers us a school of learning, and we are constantly given opportunities to grow and expand.

In every challenging situation, there is always a gift to be found. It may be that you have received insights or deeper wisdom, extra strength, or a new pathway in life.

Have you ever felt that you didn't get something you thought you wanted more than anything, only to find that something better came along? And have you noticed that whenever you experience trauma, in one form or another, it can make you stronger as a result?

HEALING DIFFICULT OR CHALLENGING SITUATIONS

To help heal and transform difficult or challenging situations, it is always helpful to ask, 'What is the gift in this situation?'

Perhaps you now understand someone better, or have seen things from another point of view. Perhaps you have grown stronger, or have learned how to avoid getting into a similar situation in the future. Or perhaps you are now ready to welcome something new into your life—a relationship, an event, or maybe a possession.

LOOKING FOR THE GIFT

When you are deeply traumatised, it is hard to see the gift or blessing offered. I'm not saying that the gift makes the event tolerable in all situations, but it may help you move through the challenge, reclaim your strength and power, or move on to a new phase of your life.

However, you also need to accept that you are human. Traumatic events or changes in your life can be stressful, and it usually takes some time to process emotions, start to cope and understand before you can look for the gift offered.

Three steps are outlined here to help you heal and cope with whatever has happened and take positive action.

STEPS TO HELP YOU COPE WITH CHALLENGING SITUATIONS

STEP 1: Send love and healing light
◇ Spend a few moments breathing in love and healing light. As you do this, let a picture form in your mind of this flow of love and light softening all your thoughts and feelings about the situation. Let it bring you to a place of peace and calm as it soothes and opens your heart.
◇ Hold in your mind the thought that the situation will unfold in a perfect way for everyone involved, in line with the divine plan.

STEP 2: Receive higher wisdom
◇ As you continue to rest and receive healing, ask your Higher Self, the wisest aspect of who you are, to give you guidance on whatever has happened.
◇ Ask that the lessons, gifts, and opportunities offered in the situation be made clear to you.
◇ Be open to receiving wise thoughts, which may seem to drop into your mind.

STEP 3: Take the appropriate action

◇ Now that you have received healing and insights, take whatever action is appropriate to resolve the situation for the highest good of all.

◇ Taking positive action will build up your strength and help you cope.

SPIRITUAL WAKE-UP CALL

A challenge in your life can also be a spiritual wake-up call. Life presents us with many challenges and lessons necessary for our spiritual growth. When you are able to see and acknowledge the gifts or lessons offered, you may discover that the experience has served its purpose and you can move on, or that circumstances in your life have changed for the better.

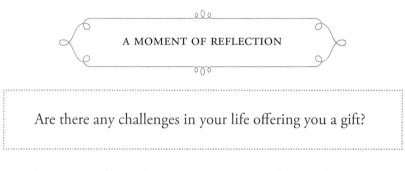

A MOMENT OF REFLECTION

Are there any challenges in your life offering you a gift?

I am grateful for all the experiences in my life that have enabled me to emerge strong, compassionate and loving.

MY STORY: GIFTS I RECEIVED FROM A CHALLENGING EVENT

My journey with a health issue brought many unexpected gifts and opportunities, and many amazing things happened.

I was quite shocked when I heard that an artery in my heart was becoming clogged and that I needed to have a stent inserted to hold it open. After the surgery I decided to take some time off work, and rented a cottage in a beautiful place in the heart of nature, by the ocean. It was an incredible gift just to be able to walk along green laneways and sandy beaches and meditate. I had time to look at the obstacles in my life, both present issues and old hurts from the past, and let them go. This opened a doorway to wonderful healing.

During this time I received the unexpected gift of writing a training course on healing with sacred sound, based on the healing work I was doing for myself. I had many insights about how positive thoughts can heal and carry everything to a new level. When I emerged from my time out, I was ready to branch out into a whole new area of teaching, based on what I had written. These gems of wisdom ignited the spark for writing this book.

The whole experience served as a very clear spiritual wake-up call, and a time for me to realign with my soul purpose.

ONE OF LIFE'S MOST DIFFICULT TIMES — WHEN A LOVED ONE DIES

One of the most heartbreaking and difficult challenges in life is when someone we love dies. If you are facing the death of a loved one, I hope the following account of how James came to terms with his father's death will bring you comfort.

JAMES'S STORY

James was incredibly sad when he realised that his elderly dad was nearing the end of his life. A few weeks earlier he had been admitted to hospital with pneumonia, and just didn't have the energy to pull through. It was a very difficult time for James and his family.

During this time James spent a lot of time thinking about life and death, and received a huge leap forward in his understanding about the nature of life and our onward journey. Although sad and griev-ing, he knew that a new door was about to open for his dad to step through to bring him home to a place where all earthly illnesses fade away and his soul could shine.

THE DIVINE PLAN FOR YOUR LIFE

As you continue to grow and evolve on your journey to enlight-enment, you will start to take life's hurdles in your stride. You will become more accepting and understanding of there being a divine plan, and you can begin to look for the opportunities, lessons and gifts in what has happened.

The next step is to take whatever action is appropriate to resolve the situation for the highest good of all.

There is a divine plan for us all, and some of the challenges in our lives have been called forward by our souls to help us grow. Say the prayer below, and allow the words to fill you with strength.

 I ask that my life unfold with grace and ease, in a perfect way, and for the highest good of all.

See the best in everyone

 Today I open my heart and let my light and love shine out, enfolding everyone I meet with love and acceptance.

Seeing the best in everyone, acknowledging their uniqueness and divinity, is an attractive force, which draws out their magnificence.

Whenever you are critical of someone, or you judge someone, look again. See the real person, exactly as they are. Know that this person is just like you, with their own hopes, dreams and challenges. They are human, and have many challenges to face. They make mistakes just as you do.

Let us be kind to each other, because we are not always aware of the stresses or challenges others face.

See the best in everyone and bless them with love and acceptance. Even if their words or actions are not loving, acknowledge that they are divine beings of light and love. Recognising their light draws out their magnificence.

Acceptance and love heals disharmony and resolves conflict. Of course, discernment is always important. Being accepting and loving doesn't mean you won't take appropriate action or say what needs to be said, but it is important that you do so in the most loving way possible.

When we feel loved and supported, we feel safe to grow, experiment and try out new things. We then let our true selves be seen.

A BEAUTIFUL THOUGHT FOR THE DAY

Let your love and light shine on everyone you meet.

Hold the thought 'I greet the Light within you' as you prepare to meet someone or pass them by.

Divine communication

You can speak in the language of the Angels—golden words of love, encouragement and support.

Your voice is a wonderful gift. It allows you to communicate about all aspects of life, to ask questions, and to express your needs. Above all, it is a magnificent and powerful tool for expressing divine frequencies of love.

Your communication, whether voiced aloud or silently, can be golden. Divine communication involves choosing words that express love, respect and appreciation for yourself and others.

Let your thoughts, spoken internally, be in the language of the Angels. As you express your thoughts, your communication becomes divine.

THE LANGUAGE OF THE ANGELS

Just holding the thought, 'Let everything I think and say be in the language of the Angels, golden words of love, encouragement and support' automatically lightens your energy, and takes you effortlessly into the flow of divine communication. Thus you can send a stream of light and love on the sound of your voice, uplifting not only yourself, but everyone around you.

A NEW GOLDEN ERA OF DIVINE COMMUNICATION

As we move towards this new era of enlightenment, love and peace, one of our biggest challenges lies in our interaction with each other. We are all incredibly unique, and have many different thoughts and opinions about all aspects of life.

It is so important to watch the words you use:
◇ Are they infused with love and acceptance?
◇ Do they support, encourage and empower?
◇ Do your words express the fullness of who you are, the beauty of your soul?

The language of love, encouragement and support is the key to creating the new golden era.

LISTENING TO OTHERS

Divine communication also involves listening to others with a view to understanding their point of view. Love is the key to empathy and understanding, which ultimately dissolves barriers and enhances relationships.

When we hold firm opinions, or deep emotions get in the way, our communication can quickly shut down. To overcome this, and ensure that our communication is infused with love, it is helpful to take a few moments to pause and review before speaking. Six steps are outlined below for ensuring that your communication is loving, golden and divine.

STEPS FOR INFUSING YOUR COMMUNICATION WITH LOVE

1. Is there someone in your life you struggle with, or something you are having difficulty expressing? It is always helpful to pause, take a step back, and give yourself time to breathe and formulate what you want to say.

2. It is important to be open to the other person's opinion. Try to be flexible and take on board the other person's point of view. Add it to your own, and consider how this might change your perception, or what you want. If you find yourself judging someone, stop and remember that love brings understanding as it dissolves barriers.

3. Choose words that are empowering and based on love. If you are feeling upset or emotional, don't infuse what you are about to say with this energy.

4. Write down what you want to communicate and reflect on it. Does this represent the truth of the situation? Our understanding is usually based on our perception of reality and our past experiences, so it is helpful to go deeper and look for the highest truth.

5. Again, take a few minutes to review everything and practice what you want to say.

6. To lift the whole situation to a higher level and infuse it with love, it generally helps to start the conversation by acknowledging something positive about the situation or person, or what you appreciate about them, before expressing what you would like to change or happen.

Your words will now be golden and divine.

THE VOICE OF YOUR HIGHER SELF

You have another powerful tool at your disposal, the voice of your Higher Self. There may be many times when you just don't know what to say in difficult situations. For example, what could be the most helpful words when someone is upset, angry or grieving. At other times you may be so annoyed or upset yourself that it can be difficult to formulate kind and loving words.

During these times you can call on the wisdom and guidance of your Higher Self, and ask a simple question: 'What would my Higher Self say in this moment?' Then, let your voice emerge from this level of wisdom.

 Within you lives a beautiful soul — your divine spark. Let each word you speak be an expression of your beauty, purity and perfection.

SPEAKING YOUR TRUTH

The most beautiful and powerful sound is the sound of your voice, the resonance of your communication. But from time to time, do you find it difficult to speak your truth?

We all recognise the truth when it is spoken and the truth holds an energy which commands respect.

Wouldn't it be wonderful if we lived in a world where we could all communicate our truth safely, knowing that our opinions would be honoured? You can contribute to this kind of world by choosing to speak in a way that respects other people's opinions and choices. As soon as we recognise that we are amazingly unique, surrounded by a remarkable diversity of people and opinions contributing to the whole, we can give ourselves and others the permission to express our true voices.

MY STORY: THE COURAGE TO SPEAK THE TRUTH

Many years ago when I took part in a healing course, it was clear from the beginning that a few of the conditions weren't quite right.

On many occasions the room was cold and draughty. As well as that, there were so many students the tutor couldn't give each person the attention they needed. Naturally, the group was dissatisfied with the course.

During the break on one particularly chilly evening, several of the students started to talk about sending a complaint to the course supervisor. Even though at the time I was very shy, I found the courage to speak up and asked that we talk to our tutor about it before sending in a written complaint. This would have been the better course of action, but more difficult than sending an anonymous letter. Unfortunately, the others didn't agree with me, and the letter was sent.

It is sad the only person who didn't know about the unrest and complaints at the time was our tutor. I have no doubt that she would have been very understanding and open to what the students needed. Worse still, I suspect she had actually heard everything that had been said—when she came back after the break there were tears in her eyes.

Many years later, looking back through the eyes of greater wisdom, I regret that I didn't speak to the tutor myself, even if the others didn't want to join me. Speaking the truth, while sometimes difficult, is the only way to achieve true understanding.

HONEST COMMUNICATION

I have learned a lot from my good friend June about how to express myself in ways that others can truly hear. The key is to use words that don't offend or trigger other people's emotions, especially fear or anger.

June and I have a deep friendship, and when something difficult is happening in our lives we take time to talk and listen to each other.

Our communication is always respectful. We don't judge, we just listen, all with a view to understanding one another.

It is amazing that when people feel heard and understood, tension and discord fade away and a space is created where people can meet each other in harmony.

 Your communication can be like leaving a trail of fresh flowers, shining with light and beauty.

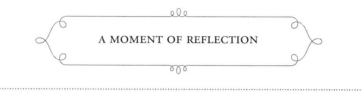

A MOMENT OF REFLECTION

Are there any areas in your life where you hold back from speaking your truth out of fear of causing offence, being judged, or rejected?

Are there any steps you can take to help yourself speak honestly and express your truth?

Let your voice express the beauty of who you are—the light of your soul.

Creating abundance

 Feeling fulfilled, rich with love, joy and abundance, is your natural state of being.

We often only associate abundance with wealth and possessions, but abundance involves all areas of our lives, including love, happiness, friendships, peace, health and success. We live in a loving Universe, and we can tap into its flow of energy to help make our dreams a reality.

It is important to nurture abundant thoughts, as these powerful seeds of creation allow even more abundance to come to you. What you focus your attention on grows and flows with the energy of conscious creation. When we ask for something to manifest for the highest good of all, we operate from a higher level. We also need to be open to receiving something other than what we expressly desire, because often there is something even better in store for us that fits with the Divine Plan.

The steps for creating abundance in your life, while working with Divine Law, are outlined below.

STEPS FOR CREATING ABUNDANCE

1. Be clear about what you want to manifest in your life. Clarity is key. This sets powerful energies in motion; the Spiritual Laws, the Law of Attraction, and your own energy.

2. Deal with any issues and clutter that may be blocking your abundance. To make space for something new to come in,

clear away the clutter of past behaviour, or thoughts about being undeserving.

3.   Ask for the abundance you want to create in your life to be for your highest good, and to support your soul growth. Ask your Higher Self, your Angels, Guides, Saints and Ascended Masters to support you in manifesting your vision in the best way.

4.   Align yourself with the vibration of abundance. You can do this by imagining you already have what you want. For instance, if you want to get a new job, think about deserving the perfect and most rewarding job for you. Imagine yourself in this role, and let all the feelings of happiness and fulfilment envelop you.

5.   Relax, knowing that the Universe is abundant in all ways, and wonderful new things are on their way to you.

Pause and review

Take a breath and pause. Spend a few minutes reviewing your experience of the various exercises in this section.

 What exercises did you particularly enjoy?

 Make a note of the wise thoughts or insights you received.

 Do you feel lighter and more joyful?

 If you put everything you have learned so far into practice in your daily life, how different do you think your life would be?

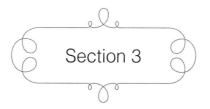

Section 3

A constant source of love and support

There is an infinite flow of love throughout the Universe—a great pool of divine light you can call upon at any time. There is no need to ever feel alone.

As we discussed briefly in the last section, you can call on your Higher Self and your Angels, Guides, Saints and Ascended Masters to help you with any challenges in your life and accelerate your spiritual growth and journey to inner peace, happiness and enlightenment.

I have recorded two guided journeys to help you merge with the light of your Higher Self, and receive a golden cloak of Angelic light. See page vi for details.

Your Higher Self

 I align with the highest aspect of who I AM, my Higher Self, and ask that I be guided by the wisdom and light of my soul.

I AM divine light
I AM infinite beauty
I AM wisdom
I AM pure love

This is who I AM — a radiant being of love and light.

I AM statements are very powerful. They align you with the mighty energies of your Higher Self and acknowledge who you truly are. For instance, when you state 'I AM divine light' this means that the quality of divine light is already a part of who you are.

YOUR HIGHER SELF — A CONSTANT SOURCE OF LOVE AND SUPPORT

Like most of us, do you often look outside yourself for guidance or solutions to difficulties? It feels good to be supported by family and friends. However, there is a constant source of love, support and guidance available to you from your Higher Self. This is the highest and wisest aspect of who you are, and your inner guiding light.

Your Higher Self will always prompt you to take action based on the highest perspective, and in the most loving way possible. Your Higher Self is aligned with the light of your soul, and holds the divine perfection of who you are — a being of great light, love, joy and deepest wisdom.

As you connect with your Higher Self, you will become aware of the full truth of who you are. This will bring an understanding of the 'oneness' within creation, and a true knowing that we are all connected on the deeper level of our souls.

ACCELERATING YOUR SPIRITUAL GROWTH

As your journey to enlightenment involves living a joyful, loving, and harmonious life, you can accelerate your spiritual growth and journey by aligning yourself with the light, wisdom and guidance of your Higher Self.

 When you step into the highest aspect of who you are, your life and relationships flow true, and miracles happen.

ACCESSING THE WISDOM AND GUIDANCE OF YOUR HIGHER SELF

You can ask your Higher Self to oversee your life in many ways.

◇ The start of the day is a particularly good time to merge with the wondrous energy of your Higher Self. Ask to be guided by the light and wisdom of your Higher Self.

◇ You can also send the light and love of your Higher Self out ahead of you each day so that everything will unfold with divine perfection.

◇ In any challenging situation, ask yourself, 'How would my Higher Self deal with this?' The answer or action to take will always be based on love. You can also ask your Higher Self to light up your aura with the highest possibilities, so that your radiance will shine on everyone involved and smooth the way forward.

◇ To receive healing, ask the light of your Higher Self to shine throughout every aspect of your being, filling you with love, light and divine frequencies, returning you to perfect balance and harmony on all levels.

◇   Ask your Higher Self to oversee your thoughts and actions, and help you see the divine perfection in everyone and in all situations.

◇   At the end of the day, review all that has happened as if you are your Higher Self. Look at any challenges that occurred. Is there anything you could have done differently? Now that you are looking at the situation from the highest perspective, is there any action you can take to resolve whatever has happened?

MERGING WITH YOUR HIGHER SELF — THE LIGHT OF YOUR SOUL

What follows is the full script of a guided journey to help you access and connect with your Higher Self. Through reading the words of this journey, you will align with the higher light of your soul and allow your Higher Self to speak to you. I advise you to read each paragraph, then pause to absorb the energy, and follow the instructions given.

As an alternative to this, as it is such a powerful journey, it is helpful to be guided through the whole process, and so I have made a recording of this meditation for you. See page vi for details.

GUIDED JOURNEY TO MERGE WITH YOUR HIGHER SELF

I invite you to take a journey in the meditation below. You will merge with the light, love and wisdom of your Higher Self, your guiding light and mighty I AM presence. You can ask a question and receive guidance on the next steps on your pathway to enlightenment, or how you can be of service to others.

1.   *Preparation for the journey*
     This is a time for you to relax and be at peace. To prepare to go on this journey, take a few moments to get yourself comfortable. Find a nice quiet place where you won't be disturbed.

You might like to light a candle, and get yourself warm and snug. Wrap yourself up in a cosy blanket, and put a pillow or cushion behind your head so you can rest back into its softness and support.

To ensure that you are fully grounded and connected to the highest source of love and light, take a moment to focus on your feet and your connection with the Earth. Imagine golden roots going right down from the soles of your feet into the Earth, growing and spreading as they hold you down solidly and securely, like the roots of a great oak tree.

Ask for a golden ray from the heart of God or the cosmos to totally surround you in a bubble of radiant light, love and wisdom. Your aura is surrounded by this high frequency light, and you are totally protected.

2. *Connect to the divine spark within your heart*
    As you start your journey to merge with your Higher Self, take your awareness to your heart area in the centre of your chest, and to your divine spark which resides there.

    Focus on your breath, and let your breathing be soft and gentle, like the waves of the ocean, flowing in and out, ever so gently and evenly.

    As you continue your gentle breathing, allow yourself to connect deeper and deeper to the bright spark of light within your heart. This is your divine essence, your centre of love, joy, and wisdom. It is the light of your soul.

    Take your time and continue to breathe in these qualities—breathing in love, joy, wisdom and light. Rest here for a while, and enjoy the feelings of well-being and deep relaxation.

3. *Merge with your Higher Self*
   Spend some time bathing in the clear light of who you truly are—bathing in divine light, beauty, wisdom and pure love. Bathe in the radiant light of your own divine essence.

   As you acknowledge who you truly are, you start to merge with your divine essence. Call upon the light of your Higher Self to merge fully with you. Perhaps you would like to say these words:

   I call my Higher Self forward to merge fully with who I am.

4. *The radiant light of your Higher Self*
   As you call your Higher Self to you, see before you a bright light. This is the light of your Higher Self, radiant and full of many colours.

   What colours can you see? Vibrant colours of the rainbow, soft pastels? Or perhaps colours that you are not so familiar with; higher frequency translucent or pearlescent colours, tinged with silver and gold.

   Perhaps you can also hear sacred sounds of soft music or chanting, or see sacred geometric shapes and symbols around you.

5. *Merging with your Higher Self*
   Now, softly and gently, see yourself moving towards your Higher Self and merging with your Higher Self.

   This is a very special moment. It is like walking into a soft cloud of rainbow light which completely surrounds you with incredible peace and love, and an expansion that's simply indescribable.

   You are completely encompassed by the many frequencies and qualities of divine light—pure love, joy, wisdom, compassion and peace. Breathe in these qualities and allow your Higher Self to fill you with the light of your soul.

This is who you are — a radiant being of light and love, merged with your Higher Self, the highest and wisest aspect of who you are.

You can rest here for a while and absorb the light of your Higher Self, as every cell and system in your body, and every layer of your aura, lights up with higher light, wisdom and love. You receive deep healing.

6. *A bridge of unity and oneness*
   You have expanded so much. Your aura is radiant, and you get a sense of your connection with everyone and everything — a sense of oneness, harmony with all, and complete unity.

   Can you imagine your Higher Self forming a bridge of light with the Higher Selves of your family and friends? Now reach out further, and connect your light to everyone you know and those you haven't yet met, bringing you a deeper understanding and awareness of the unique and special people in your life.

   We are all mighty beings of light, love and wisdom. We are all connected, all part of the oneness, and all part of the divine plan.

   As you realise this, your whole being is lighting up with the highest possibilities for yourself, and your true potential. Take a few minutes to rest as this light rises to the surface, illuminating who you truly are.

7. *Your pathway to enlightenment*
   Now you are aware of the light and love of your Higher Self in your life. Your Higher Self can guide you on the next steps to

take on your journey to enlightenment. There may be a question that you would like to ask this all seeing and wise aspect of yourself. This may be the most important question of your life.

Perhaps you would like to ask:
◇   What is the next step on my journey to enlightenment?
◇   What is my highest pathway this lifetime?
◇   How can I be of service and show others the way?

Ask your question and allow the answer to flow into your mind. You may receive inspiration through wise thoughts dropping into your mind, or through images and pictures. You may be aware of colours or sacred shapes and symbols, or perhaps deep feelings of love and peace. Whatever answer you receive is perfect for you, and will guide you in the direction of the next step, or steps, to take on your journey.

8.   *Your Higher Self will continue to guide and bless you*
Take a moment to ask your Higher Self to oversee your life and to continue to guide you to live in love, light and wisdom.

As you do this, you might like to say this prayer:

PRAYER TO MY HIGHER SELF

I align myself with the highest aspect of
who I AM, my Higher Self, and ask that
I be guided by the wisdom and light of my soul.

I ask my Higher Self to oversee my thoughts
and actions, today and in the future,
and help me see the divine perfection
in everyone and in all situations.

If you wish, you can send divine light out ahead of you to shine love and light on everything you do and everyone you meet today. That way, all will unfold perfectly.

Know that you can align with the radiance of your Higher Self, the light of your soul, at any time. All you need to do is ask your Higher Self to oversee your life, and be willing to live your life based on lightness and joy, love and wisdom.

Now that you have taken this journey, you may notice that wise thoughts continue to drop into your mind over the next few days, and many amazing and magical synchronicities occur.

9. *Completing the journey*
Finish by taking a moment or two to thank your Higher Self for this experience, and for enfolding you in love, light and deepest wisdom.

How are you feeling? Refreshed and peaceful? Radiant with light?

As you have been so open during this journey, ask your Higher Self to place a radiant golden cloak of light all around you, totally enclosing your aura and protecting you. You will then continue to hold all the love, peace, joy and wisdom close to you.

Bring your focus back to your feet, and sense or imagine the golden roots, like the roots of a great oak tree, growing and spreading as they hold you solidly and securely on the Earth once more. As you do this, you may be aware of your feet getting heavier, like anchors.

You might like to rest for a while to fully absorb all that you have received, then finish by stretching gently.

MY EXPERIENCE OF MERGING WITH MY HIGHER SELF

Everyone experiences this journey in their own unique way. I was surrounded by the light of my Higher Self in a triangle of rainbow light and pearlescent colours, which filled all the cells of my body. I received deep healing, and felt rejuvenated and balanced again.

All concerns faded away and were transformed. I had complete trust in my Higher Self to guide and look after me, and to orchestrate experiences that would best serve my highest good. It was a step on my journey that brought me closer to unity and enlightenment.

I AM what I AM.
The divine in me recognises the divine in you.

Angels will light your way

 Angels guide amazing and magical synchronicities to light up your life.

Angels are aspects of divine consciousness and a bridge between mankind and God. They have a light and joyful energy, and are willing to help us in every way possible. They particularly love to assist us in awakening our own angelic qualities of love, joy, peace and abundance—all the qualities of enlightenment. When we are full of these qualities, life flows so much smoother, and we are able to share our love and joy with others.

MY STORY: MY EXPERIENCES OF ANGELIC ASSISTANCE

When I first started working with Angels, there were times I wondered if what happened when I asked for guidance was really brought about by the Angels, or just coincidence. But the experiences I have had when I ask for help have shown me that it is much more than coincidence.

I have found that when I ask for help, my requests are always answered. Sometimes help or guidance is given directly, or at other times indirectly, such as being guided to a book which holds the answer, hearing something really helpful on radio or TV, or through a friend giving me just the right information or offer of help at the right time.

When I ask the Angels for assistance, for the highest outcome, they then set up magical synchronicities, or drop wise thoughts into my mind guiding me to the next step, or another way of tackling a problem. Sometimes the answer is revealed in a dream.

GUARDIAN ANGELS

We each have our own Guardian Angel. Always by our side, our Angel enfolds us in love and compassion, while lovingly guiding us and easing any challenges we may face.

You may be aware of your Angel's presence by sensing their peace and love around you. You may see a colour with your inner vision, or perhaps you may smell their wonderful perfume. You may even be aware of the gentle energy of your Angel, light tingling sensations, or a warm or cool gentle flow of air.

MEET YOUR GUARDIAN ANGEL

Would you like to develop an even closer relationship with your Angel? You can do this by following the steps outlined below, and you can ask your Angel for assistance with any worries or challenges in your life. Your prayers and requests are always heard.

STEPS FOR MEETING YOUR GUARDIAN ANGEL

1. Find a nice quiet place where you won't be disturbed and get yourself warm and comfortable. You might like to light a candle and play peaceful and relaxing music.

2. Close your eyes and imagine that you are in a special meeting place, perhaps a beautiful garden or a magical place in nature.

3. Invite your Guardian Angel to step in close to you and enfold you in his/her wings.

4.   Imagine your Angel inviting you to rest back in his/her loving arms. Rest there for a few moments, and notice how you are feeling.

5.   You can talk to your Angel about any worries or troubles you have, and ask your compassionate guardian to ease whatever is happening in your life and help you find the best solutions.

6.   Rest for a few minutes. In this quiet moment you may even hear the promptings of your Angel, which may seem like wise thoughts dropping into your mind. Your Angel will always find a way to assist you, in the best possible manner.

7.   Thank your Angel.

Your Guardian Angel will be delighted to stay by your side, lovingly guiding and assisting you. Please keep in mind that your Angel likes you to ask for their assistance, as under spiritual law, your Angel will never interfere with your free will.

ARCHANGELS

There are many thousands of Archangels who have various roles. They serve in a cosmic capacity, and also assist us in our day-to-day lives. As love, protection, healing and guidance are primary concerns for most people, there is a brief outline of the Archangels who oversee these areas below.

ARCHANGEL CHAMUEL AND THE ANGELS OF LOVE

When you call on Archangel Chamuel and the Angels of Love, they will surround you with their loving energies. The Angels of Love will help dissolve and heal sadness, pain, or grief in your heart, and make your thoughts peaceful, with love and joy where there once was hurt. They will assist you to find your soulmate, and they also help heal relationships so that love can flow again.

ARCHANGEL MICHAEL, THE ANGEL OF PROTECTION

You can ask Archangel Michael to protect you in any situation. He will step in close to you and surround you with his deep blue cloak of protection, keeping you safe and shielding you from all harm and negative influences. You can also ask him to protect your family, children, friends, pets, or your property. Archangel Michael will spread his protective light wherever you request it.

ARCHANGEL RAPHAEL AND THE ANGELS OF HEALING

Archangel Raphael and the Angels of Healing have enormous compassion. When you ask them for healing, your prayers are always heard, and they will do whatever they can for your highest good. They dissolve any stuck energy or emotions which are causing ill health, and they help strengthen positive qualities to bring out the best in you. The Angels are also delighted to work with you to help heal other people, places and situations.

ARCHANGEL GABRIEL AND THE ANGELS OF GUIDANCE

During your quiet time or meditation, you can ask Archangel Gabriel and the Angels of Guidance to help you find the next step on your life's path. They will light up the symbols of your life's work within your aura, so that doors open effortlessly and you attract the perfect people and opportunities to you. Archangel Gabriel is also well known for protecting mothers during childbirth.

GOLDEN ANGELIC CLOAK OF LIGHT

This is a beautiful exercise which is ideal for the start of the day, or whenever you feel under pressure. You can ask your Angels to surround you with a golden cloak of Angelic light, which will soothe and calm your thoughts and emotions, while filling you with lightness and joy. Your golden Angelic cloak of light will ensure that everything you touch, see, hear, say and do, will be for the highest good of all.

The Angels work with the colour gold, as it has a very high vibration, holding the qualities of wisdom, love, and peace. As they surround you with a golden cloak of light, you will be uplifted to hold these qualities, and you will have an enormous effect on people around you.

ASK THE ANGELS TO SURROUND YOU WITH A GOLDEN ANGELIC
CLOAK AND BECOME THE ANGEL OF LIGHT THAT YOU ARE

Ask the Angels to give you *golden hands*—
so that everything you TOUCH will be for the highest good.

Ask the Angels to give you *golden eyes*—
so that everything you SEE will be for the highest good.

Ask the Angels to give you *golden ears*—
so that everything you HEAR will be for the highest good.

Ask the Angels to give you a *golden mouth*—
so that everything you SAY will be for the highest good.

Ask the Angels to give you *golden feet*—
so that everything you DO will be for the highest good.

And ask the Angels to totally *surround you in a golden cloak*—
so that everything you ARE today will be for the highest good.

You can share this energy with everyone you meet. Wearing your golden cloak of light, you will find yourself talking kindly to everyone and letting the light of love, compassion and understanding shine from your eyes towards every person, thing, or situation you encounter. Everyone and everything you come into contact with will be uplifted by your golden stream of love.

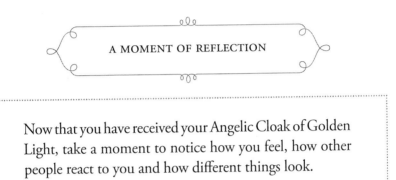

A MOMENT OF REFLECTION

Now that you have received your Angelic Cloak of Golden Light, take a moment to notice how you feel, how other people react to you and how different things look.

Saints and Ascended Masters

 Saints and Ascended Masters are highly evolved divine beings, who hold great light.

Just as there are many thousands of Angels that we can call on for assistance, there are also many Saints and Ascended Masters who hold various roles in the Universe. When we call them to us, they surround us with many blessings and do whatever they can to assist and guide us on our journey to enlightenment.

You may already have an affinity with a particular Saint or Ascended Master. I have listed below some of the enlightened beings who are best known to us, along with their roles and service to humanity.

JESUS CHRIST
— Beams cosmic love to everyone.

MOTHER MARY
— Brings grace, wisdom and compassion.

PADRE PIO
— A miracle worker.

ST ANTHONY
— Finds lost articles.

ST FRANCIS OF ASSISI
— Patron Saint of Animals.

MELCHIZEDEK
— Brings forward ancient wisdom.

ST GERMAIN
— Transformation with the Violet Flame.

GAUTAMA BUDDHA
— Brings peace, wisdom and illumination.

LORD KUTHUMI
— Teaches us about spiritual truths and enlightenment.

QUAN YIN
— Unconditional love, represents the divine feminine.

SERAPIS BEY
— Brings harmony, balance and the ancient wisdom of Egypt.

In the next section, I will guide you through the steps for inviting a team of divine beings to come into your life to support and assist you.

A team to support you

 There are an incredible number of divine beings in service to our Universe, who are willing to step forward and assist you, all you need do is ask.

Now that you have explored how to connect with the wisdom and guidance of your Higher Self, Angels, Saints and Ascended Masters, you may wish to call on a particular team to support you. You may have a special project in mind that you would like support with, or perhaps you would like healing and guidance to accelerate your spiritual growth and journey to inner peace, happiness and enlightenment.

CALLING ON A TEAM TO SUPPORT YOU

The steps for inviting a team of divine beings to support you are straightforward.

1. Ensure that you are grounded and protected by focusing on your feet on the floor and visualise golden roots holding you firmly on the Earth. Then, ask Archangel Michael to place his deep blue cloak of protection around you.

2. Ask for pure divine light to flow throughout your mind and body, purifying your mind so your thoughts will be clear and bright, and you will be open to hearing the wise promptings of your divine guides.

3. Visualise a beautiful meeting place, a special place in nature where you are comfortable and relaxed. Say a prayer, stating the

assistance you would like to receive, and ask the Angels, Guides, Saints and Ascended Masters to come forward to support you.

4. You may receive a name or names, or be aware of a colour or sensation, or deep feelings of love and joy, as your team of divine beings step in close to you. This is to let you know they are there, supporting you.

5. Thank your team for their support.

It is a good idea to set aside time each day to meditate or pray, so you are open to hear the wise guidance of your team.

 Angels, Saints and Ascended Masters assist you on your journey to enlightenment.

Pause and review

Pause and take some time to review your experience of working with the information within this section.

 Did you find it helpful to connect with your Higher Self and the Angels, Saints and Ascended Masters?

 Make a note of any insights or new information you received.

 Write down any changes you are planning to make.

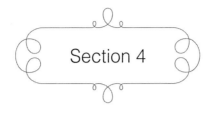

Section 4

Spiritual practice

Taking time each day to still your mind and focus on enlightening words, sacred texts and prayer, is important for your overall well-being. Many ways of calming your mind and meditating are included in this section, along with beautiful prayers and inspirational words. The spiritual words will uplift your soul to higher levels of lightness and joy.

Meditation will take you into the still, silent place at the centre of your being, where you can hear the wise promptings of your soul guiding you on your journey of growth. May you be blessed on your journey.

Meditation

Meditation is the way to bring us back to ourselves, where
we can really experience and taste our full being.
—Sogyal Rinpoche

Meditation is a process where you can still your mind and bring your
focus inward, entering a state of peace and calm. From this sacred
place within, you can touch the essence of who you truly are; the
light of your soul, the part of you that is already enlightened.

When you meditate, you are more open to hear the promptings
of your wise inner voice, and the guidance of your Angels, Guides,
Saints and Ascended Masters.

On a physical level, meditation gives your body and mind time to
return to balance and harmony. It has many health benefits—it
soothes stress and headaches, reduces blood pressure, helps you sleep
well, and gives your body time to heal on all levels.

STILLING YOUR MIND

There are many ways of training your mind to become more peaceful,
which is the essence of meditation. But it is important to understand that your mind is never without thought. Thoughts are part
of who you are, and you are constantly assessing what is happening
around you. You can, however, try to simply notice your thoughts
without giving them too much attention or trying to force them
from your mind.

These are the words I often use when guiding people to quieten their mind in meditation:

> Focus on the sound and rhythm of your breath. Let your thoughts be like the soft puffy clouds drifting across the sky. Notice your thoughts as they come into your mind, but don't give them any attention. Let them drift from your mind again. See them moving on, so you can once again focus on the sound and rhythm of your breath.

A FOCUS FOR YOUR MIND

It is always helpful to give your mind something gentle to focus on; for instance, a candle flame, a flower or a beautiful image. You can also focus on words with high vibrations which can soothe and relax you as they fill you with their light. A single word or a short sentence which you say repeatedly is ideal, and will replace the clutter of thoughts with a single focus.

Before starting to meditate, keep in mind a few points:
◇ Make sure you are comfortable, warm, and have a blanket nearby, as your body temperature may drop when you relax and meditate.
◇ Keep your spine straight so that your energy can flow freely.
◇ Aim to meditate for between twenty to thirty minutes every day. It is easier to start with ten minutes a day and build up your practice.

THERE ARE MANY WAYS TO MEDITATE

We have already discussed some of the ways of stilling your mind and entering a meditative state. The suggestions below will help you to put this into practice.

STILLING YOUR MIND WITH YOUR BREATH

Focusing on the rhythm of your breath slows your mind and body, and helps you keep a clear, centred focus.

1. Breathe in and out, slowly and evenly, noticing the rhythm of your breath.

2. Count your breaths, from one to ten, then start again.

An alternative to counting is to focus on the rhythm of your breath while holding an image in your mind of ocean waves rolling to shore, then flowing out again, to the rhythm of your breath.

CANDLE MEDITATION

1. Focus on the flame of a candle. Notice its size, shape and colour as it flickers and changes.

2. After a minute or two, close your eyes and imagine the flame is now within your third eye, at the centre of your forehead.

3. Imagine this is the light of your soul or Higher Self, and it is filling you with its light.

SACRED WORDS

1. Start by focusing on the rhythm of your breath.

2. Repeat sacred words of a prayer or chant, or you can choose your own words. For example, one well-known chant is *Om Mani Padme Hum* — an ancient Sanskrit mantra meaning 'the divine resides in the centre of my heart'. Alternatively, you could focus on single words; for instance, wisdom, love, joy or peace.

3. Let the energy of the words fill you with their high vibration and light.

MEDITATE ON THE LIGHT OF YOUR SOUL

1. Start by focusing on the rhythm of your breath.

2. Then focus on the love (or the divine spark) within your heart.

3. Imagine the loving feeling (or your divine spark) expanding and totally surrounding you in an oval of light.

4. Imagine a door opening in front of you, and a great being of light walks towards you. This is the energy of your Higher Self—the light of your soul.

5. Continue to focus on the rhythm of your breath, while drawing in the energy of your Higher Self and merging with this wondrous light.

> The gift of learning to meditate is the greatest gift you can give yourself in this life. For it is only through meditation that you can undertake the journey to discover your true nature, and so find the stability and confidence you will need to live, and die, well. Meditation is the road to enlightenment.
> —Sogyal Rinpoche, *The Tibetan Book of Living and Dying*

Prayers and inspirational words

> Prayer makes your heart bigger, until it is capable of containing the gift of God himself.
> —Mother Teresa

Prayers, inspirational words and blessings are spoken from the heart to communicate with God or a higher power, ask for divine intervention and assistance, or give thanks for what we already have. Their uplifting words comfort and enrich our lives, and take us further on our journey to enlightenment.

Everyone has their own favourite prayers or inspirational words.

Let the words speak to your heart and soul and enfold you in love.

The following prayer is one of my favourites, as it encompasses the ethos of all faiths and religions. I regard it as a prayer of enlightenment. The prayer is attributed to St Francis of Assisi, Patron Saint of animals and founder of the Franciscan Order in the 13th century. It is based on his life and teachings. The words are inspirational, and contain deep spiritual truths. Although written many centuries ago, the messages are still relevant for us today.

PRAYER OF ST FRANCIS OF ASSISI

Lord, make me an instrument of Your peace
Where there is hatred, let me sow love
Where there is injury, pardon

Where there is doubt, faith
Where there is despair, hope
Where there is darkness, light
Where there is sadness, joy.

O Divine Master,
Grant that I may not so much seek
To be consoled, as to console
To be understood, as to understand
To be loved, as to love.

For it is in giving that we receive
It is in pardoning that we are pardoned
And it is in dying that we are born to Eternal Life.
Amen.

The words of the prayer are universal. It has been recited by many world leaders throughout the ages, including Bill Clinton and Margaret Thatcher, and Mother Teresa as she received the Nobel Peace Prize in 1979. During World War II, it was widely circulated as a prayer for peace.

You might like to write your own prayers, or choose inspirational passages from the Bible or other sacred texts. Whatever prayers or inspirational words you choose to focus on, let them lift your heart and soul to new levels of light and love.

Creating a safe and sacred environment for your spiritual practice

You can create an amazing, sacred environment in your own home, filled with light, peace and tranquillity, where healing takes place as soon as you enter.

CREATING A SACRED ENVIRONMENT

It is always good to set aside a special place for your spiritual practice, meditation, or healing exercises. With a little attention to detail, you can create a beautiful and sacred environment, where you feel totally nurtured and safe.

◇ Lighting a candle symbolises the welcoming of Divine light into the space, provides an excellent focal point, and infuses your room with warm, mystical light.

◇ To freshen your room, incense, smudge sticks or sacred music will clear and cleanse any stagnant energy present.

◇ Placing crystals in your sacred space will energise it, and the crystals will add their own special healing qualities. Amethyst and Rose Quartz are good choices. Amethyst clears negative energies, while Rose Quartz helps you to open your heart, and infuses your room with the energy of love.

◇ Flowers help keep the energy in your room pure and clear, while also adding their wonderful aromas and beautiful colours.

◇ When you have set up your room, ask the Angels to surround your sacred space with a bubble of protective golden or white light, or invoke a protective light from the heart of God or the cosmos.

ATTUNING TO THE HIGHEST LIGHT

At the start of the day, or before meditating or doing healing exercises, it is helpful to attune to the highest source of light and love, while being fully grounded and protected.

Performing these simple preliminary steps ensures you will:

◇ Be firmly grounded, enabling you to connect with higher energies and bring them into your life.
◇ Connect easily with your Angels, Guides, Saints, Ascended Masters and Divine Light.
◇ Work safely with the highest possible energies.

At the end of the day, after meditating, or when your healing session is complete, it is also good practice to close down your energies, to ground and protect yourself again. This is because when you connect to higher energies or receive healing, your energetic bodies are very open and expanded. It is also important to hold your new energies in a safe way.

It can be helpful to do this before you go to sleep. It is comforting to surround your aura with a protective light so you can truly relax and let go, knowing that you are safe and protected while you rest.

STEPS FOR ATTUNING TO DIVINE LIGHT

1. You can ground yourself by visualising cords of light or magnets at the soles of your feet, holding you solidly to the Earth.

2. Attune to the highest source of light and love by asking your Higher Self, the Angels and beings of light from the spiritual

realms to watch over your life. You can ask for a large column of white or gold light to come down from God or the cosmos to completely surround you. Alternatively, you can visualise a white or gold radiant star beaming its light over you.

3. You may like to call in any qualities that you would like to be surrounded by. For example, high vibration qualities such as love, joy, peace, acceptance, clarity and confidence. These qualities of enlightenment will assist in keeping your energies clear and bright throughout the day.

4. Protect yourself by asking your Higher Self, the Angels or beings of light to place a bubble of divine light around you, golden or white. Or, you can request Archangel Michael to surround you with his deep blue cloak of protection.

At the end of the day, after meditating or after receiving healing, follow steps 1 and 4 again to ensure you are fully grounded and protected once more.

Section 5

Transformation and spiritual growth

In this section you are encouraged to lovingly step into your power and boost your confidence and self-esteem, so that you can truly honour yourself and everyone around you.

This is deep work, and I advise you to take your time. It is a good idea to revisit this section frequently, as transformative work can be like peeling an onion, layer by layer, as you heal and work through issues one by one. Peeling away the layers will give you a new freedom as old stagnant energies are removed. Your light will shine brightly, illuminating your highest pathway.

Step into your power

Our deepest fear is not that we are inadequate. Our deepest fear is that we are powerful beyond measure. It is our light, not our darkness that most frightens us. We ask ourselves, Who am I to be brilliant, gorgeous, talented, fabulous? Actually, who are you not to be? You are a child of God. Your playing small does not serve the world.
—Marianne Williamson

A lot of people do not realise just how powerful they truly are. Have you ever found yourself acting small, not allowing your true colours to be seen or voice to be heard? Many people would answer yes, as we have been conditioned to stay hidden and small so as not to create waves around us. Sometimes, we are simply gripped by fears and insecurities.

 At any stage of your life you can transform whatever is holding you back, and step fully into your power.

CONFIDENCE, ENERGY AND ENTHUSIASM

Giving your confidence a boost will give you new energy and enthusiasm to step into your power. If you feel blocked in any area of your life, follow these steps for boosting your confidence so you can reach your goals.

STEPS FOR BOOSTING CONFIDENCE

1.   Imagine the most loving person in your life is standing before

you, telling you how wonderful you are and that you deserve the best. Imagine them encouraging you to be the magnificent person that you are.

2.   Listen to what they are saying, and take a few moments to absorb the new messages.

3.   Notice how you are feeling now. Are you ready to move forward? Perhaps you feel ready to start that project you have been thinking about, or apply for that promotion you were dreaming of. You may simply be more confident in letting your light and powerful presence be seen.

After performing this quick exercise, it is always helpful to prepare a step-by-step plan of action for reaching your goals. This will help you see all the progress you are making.

Reclaiming your power and acting for the highest good accelerates your spiritual growth and journey to enlightenment.

EMPOWERING YOURSELF TO LEAD A JOYFUL AND FULFILLING LIFE

You can empower yourself at any time by the decisions and choices you make.

Three of the most important choices in our lives are:
◇   How we spend our time.
◇   Who we spend it with.
◇   Where we spend it.

Our choices are limitless. It is helpful to review these three important areas in your life and see if there is anything you would like to change, or if there is something new you would like to bring into your life. Remember, every situation can be transformed by making step-by-step changes at a pace that suits you. Formulate a very clear plan for achieving your goal, and then take the steps to reach it.

 You are a powerful person and in control of your destiny.

HEALING AND COUNSELLING

If you are finding things difficult and are feeling powerless, unfulfilled, and can't see how things can change, stop and review. Explore your thoughts, feelings, and the obstacles that may be holding you back. Talk things through with a friend or a counsellor. Make the choice to seek support and healing to help you move forward.

There is no need to be held back by any of life's experiences. Look for the gift in everything. Heal the past, and acknowledge all that you have learned along the way. Emerge as the magnificent and powerful person that you are.

ASK FOR WHAT YOU WANT

Being authentic and asking for what you truly desire allows you to take responsibility for getting what you need. This is an important step into your power.

 The greatest gift you can give to others is to be true to yourself—your happiness is contagious.

Self-worth and confidence

 Know that you are a unique and divine being, perfect from the very first day.

Low self-esteem and lack of confidence can slow down your spiritual growth. It takes away your energy and stifles you, preventing you from realising the full potential of who you are — an unlimited, radiant being of light.

The foundations of our self-worth and confidence are formed at a very young age. We are constantly picking up messages from those around us, firstly from our parents and family members, then from our experience engaging with others as we start our educational journey.

We take messages about ourselves on board, which can then become firm beliefs.

It is very helpful to look at the messages you may have picked up from others, or the beliefs you hold about yourself, and try to see the truth. For instance, one of the most prevalent messages we pick up is that we don't deserve to be loved, that we aren't good enough. This stems from experiences where we were rejected, laughed at, or didn't meet expectations.

THE SOURCE OF YOUR BELIEFS

If one of your cores beliefs is that you aren't good enough, or don't deserve to be loved, see if you can find the source of that belief. Can you remember when you first felt this way? Did someone criticise or judge you? Or were you facing a challenging time, and didn't fare as well as you would have liked?

Look back at when this belief may have first formed. How long have you held this belief? It is time to let go, and replace it with a more empowering truth.

TRANSFORMING BELIEFS

It is helpful to write down the belief that has a negative impact and erodes your confidence. Then write down the opposite. Use this second word as an affirmation, a new belief. Repeat it over and over again, so that you radiate with new, higher frequency truths.

It is time to leave the past behind. Let go of all the old patterns, ways of being and thinking. Let go of the hurts that have shaped your life, and the negative comments that you held as the truth.

Take some time to look at your core beliefs and work with the tools for transformation throughout this section to heal and let go of old thoughts, habits and beliefs, so you can reclaim the true you.

◊   The Violet Flame is particularly helpful for transmuting old patterns and beliefs.
◊   Cutting cords will help clear away attachments to negative beliefs and energies.
◊   Affirmations will help you replace negative thoughts, beliefs and realities with supportive and positive ones.
◊   The Bubble of Heavenly Light healing exercise will help you become aware of how precious you are, as you are surrounded with an oval of love and divine frequencies.

Remember, you are a divine being of light and love, and are perfect just as you are.

HEALING THE PAST WITH LOVE

You can heal wounds from the past and awaken again to love and joy. The exercise which follows takes you on a journey to meet the important people in your life, both past and present, giving you the opportunity to heal old wounds and realise how loved you actually are.

STEPS FOR HEALING PAST WOUNDS AND OPENING TO LOVE AND JOY

1. Close your eyes and relax.

2. Imagine you are standing in the centre of a beautiful serene garden, surrounded by all the important people in your life, both past and present. Perhaps some of these people hurt you deeply in the past, but today you are meeting with the higher aspects of who they are, where only love exists.

3. Each person comes forward and stands in front of you. They tell you how much they love you and also have a special message for you.

4. Open your heart and receive this love and special message. Breathe in the love, and with every breath you take, let it fill you more and more.

5. Relax for a few minutes to fully absorb all you have received.

6. Now see yourself walking around the circle. Stop in front of each person. Tell them how much you love them and see them smile, brimming with happiness.

7. When you have completed the circle, open your eyes again. Are you also smiling and happy? Do you feel a soft glow of love radiating from your heart?

CONFIDENCE BUILDING

If your self-esteem and confidence are low, you can build yourself up with the four steps for transformation suggested below.

1. Do something different a few times a week. For instance, start a night class, meet new people, or explore a new hobby. This shifts your focus from the old to new and exciting ventures and gives you a boost. Focus on how well you are doing.

2. Visualise success. Allow the energy of your positive thoughts to create successful outcomes. Embrace all the good feelings associated with this success. Visualisation is a powerful process, and supports the creation of a new reality.

3. Give yourself a positive boost at the start and finish of each day. Say positive affirmations. Fill yourself with encouraging and confident words.

4. Congratulate yourself on the areas of your life that are going well for you. We are often confident in some areas of our lives and less so in others. Know you can make progress and build confidence in the areas where you are unsure of your abilities.

BE RADIANT, CONFIDENT AND FULL OF VITALITY

Building your confidence and increasing your self-esteem puts you in a positive loop of radiance and vitality. Confidence increases the flow of endorphins, the 'happy hormones' which help you to feel even more radiant and confident. This in turn tells your body to release even more endorphins, boosting your self-esteem to higher levels and continuing the flow of good feelings.

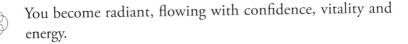 You become radiant, flowing with confidence, vitality and energy.

Transform old habits and patterns

 Step into the positive flow of goodness within the Universe, where everything is possible.

In this section, we will focus on the power of affirmations to transform old habits to new. In doing so, our mind, body and spirit will step in to support the creation of this new reality.

HOW DO AFFIRMATIONS WORK?

Repetition is the key to embedding new thoughts and beliefs within your consciousness and transforming old habits. Your brain is constantly changing in response to information it receives from your thoughts and environment.

Humans can create new neural pathways in their brains, supporting what they want to be, or what they want to create. Repetition programmes your mind the same way that exercise builds muscles. Affirmations help you achieve new realities, as repeating positive statements creates neural connections in your brain to foster new beliefs and habits.

Knowing this, you can consciously improve your well-being on all levels simply by changing your thoughts and beliefs.

Take time each day to repeat positive statements. They will lighten up your life with more joy, abundance and a sense of fulfilment.

STEPS FOR CREATING SUCCESSFUL AFFIRMATIONS

1. Affirmations are particularly helpful if you are feeling stuck or negative about an aspect of your life. It is important to choose words that affirm that whatever you want has already come to pass.

2. Starting your statement with 'I am' ensures that what you are asserting has already happened.

    For instance, if you want to lose weight, your affirmation could be: 'I am now a perfect weight,' rather than 'I want to lose three kilos over the next six weeks,' or 'I am going to lose weight over the coming months.'

    If you worry that you will never succeed in your goals, an example of a positive affirmation could be: 'I am now confident and successful in all I do.'

3. As you say your affirmation, try to truly feel what it would be like if your statement was already true. For an affirmation of confidence, imagine the feeling of being confident and successful in a project, or an area of your life. Give yourself the encouragement and permission to feel the lightness, happiness and confidence that come with it.

4. Let pictures form in your mind of how you look and act, and what you are doing now that you have achieved your goal.

5. Repeat your affirmation as often as you can, ideally setting time aside in the morning, midday and evening. You can say your affirmation as you travel to work, when you go for a walk, or while relaxing in the evening.

6. You can work with up to three affirmations at any one time, but it is best not to focus on any more than this.

7. After about seven days it may be time to ask yourself the question — 'Is there any positive action I can now take to support the new me?' This could involve trying out a new hobby, or dressing in a way that reflects your new energy.

POSITIVE QUESTIONS

Another way to formulate affirmations is to ask yourself positive questions, for instance:

'Why am I so lovable?' or 'Why am I so successful at everything I do?'

Let your heart and soul provide you with the answers, which is always an illuminating exercise. You can then turn the answers into positive statements to reinforce the message.

SAY YOUR AFFIRMATION FOR TWENTY-ONE DAYS

It can take up to twenty-one days to reprogramme your mind with a new message, and whatever you focus on becomes a new habit or belief. Can you imagine how strong your beliefs are, based on the messages you have held onto for years, or even lifetimes?

 You can start to change your beliefs and behaviours right now, and attract all the good that life has to offer.

You may find that you need to say your affirmation for less than twenty-one days and are happy with the result, or you may decide to change or adjust your affirmation and start another twenty-one day resolution.

STAYING ALIGNED WITH THE DIVINE PLAN FOR YOUR LIFE

Ask that what you are affirming comes to you in a way that is for your highest good, and the highest good of all.

In doing so, you will always stay in alignment with the divine plan for your life and spiritual laws. We can't always see the bigger picture, and sometimes there is a higher purpose in our circumstances. Holding this thought in mind allows the most appropriate outcome to unfold and leaves space for something even better to come into your life.

EXAMPLES OF AFFIRMATIONS

◊ My life is flowing with abundance, happiness and vitality.
◊ I am powerful and in control of my own destiny.
◊ I am loved and supported by my family and friends.
◊ I am radiantly happy and healthy.
◊ My thoughts nourish my mind, body and soul.
◊ I know that I am loved, and I accept love in my life right now.
◊ I now attract the perfect relationship.
◊ I am abundant, and money flows to me from many sources.
◊ I am successful at whatever I do.

Write your own positive statements. Enjoy the experience, and allow your mind, body and soul to help you create the life of your dreams.

Forgiveness

 Allow the healing light of forgiveness to shine from your heart and transform all to love.

Forgiveness is a quality of enlightenment. It is the greatest gift you can give yourself and others. It helps you to let go and heal, cutting the cords that bind you to unhappiness, dependency and destructive patterns of behaviour. As you forgive and heal old wounds and hurts, you set yourself and others free.

Forgiveness brings you the gifts of love, compassion, understanding and acceptance. It heals as it dissolves clouds of hurt and anger, and allows your love and light to shine out clearly and radiantly.

There are many situations which can be healed with forgiveness:
◇   When others have done or said hurtful things to us, forgiveness can ease and heal the situation.
◇   We can ask others to forgive us for any hurt we caused them.
◇   We need to forgive ourselves for any wrongdoing or any hurt we have caused others (and ourselves).
◇   Sometimes we need to let go, and forgive people for not giving us what we needed, or for not being who we wanted them to be.
◇   If you are holding on to a hurt, or if an event from the past is influencing your behaviour today, forgiveness is key.

When you forgive, the energy that was tied up in anger and resentment is now available to you, and you can channel this new energy into other projects and joyful activities.

STORY OF FORGIVENESS AND TRANSFORMATION

Patricia was very angry with a friend who had hurt her deeply. She hadn't felt this traumatised in years, and felt her anger was completely justified after what had happened. After a few very emotional and exhausting days, a wise friend advised her that it was time to stop letting this situation take over her life.

The breakthrough came for Patricia when she decided to try to let go of all the anger she was holding towards her friend. She wanted to try to understand what had happened from her friend's point of view, and forgive all that had been said.

First, she let a picture form in her mind of the size and shape of the anger surrounding her. She saw images of big black and red boulders connected by forks of lightning.

Patricia started to visualise the anger dissolving, and pictured the boulders changing into soft pink clouds of love. She also asked her Angels to help release the emotional blocks and tangles in her heart. It took about ten minutes for the dark boulders to transform into the soft pink of love, and as this happened, Patricia felt her heart starting to open. It was a wonderfully uplifting experience, where she felt at peace and in the flow of love again.

Patricia then visualised rays of love flowing out from her heart, carrying all the love and compassion she could give. She pictured herself and her friend totally surrounded by the pink light of unconditional love, and saw this light forming a connection between them. In this loving energy, she realised it was possible to forgive and let the situation go, freeing both herself and her friend from the sticky energy of anger.

Later that day, Patricia met her friend quite unexpectedly. Now feeling at peace, she was able to talk to her friend and express how she felt about what had happened in a very loving way. She was also able to listen to her friend with love and compassion, and they each felt heard and understood.

It usually takes just one person with an open heart to extend the hand of friendship and transform even the most difficult situation to one of love and understanding.

FORGIVING OTHERS

We all have people in our lives that we have difficulty with, or whose behaviour has affected us in the past. Perhaps these people haven't changed, or situations haven't been resolved, so we may still be holding on to hurt or resentment.

Sending forgiveness will open your heart and free up your energy, bringing you peace of mind and soul again.

STEPS FOR FORGIVING OTHERS

1. Bring to mind a person or situation in need of healing and forgiveness.

2. Imagine you are standing under a waterfall of divine love and light. The waterfall cascades around you, sparkling with gold and diamond light, and all the colours of the rainbow.

3. Say a forgiveness prayer, such as:

    I forgive you [person's name] for [whatever event]. I know you were doing the very best you could at the time. I forgive you and I set you free.

4. See the waterfall of light cascading all around you, cleansing

and transforming the old energies involving that person or situation. See your aura being filled with divine love and starting to sparkle with all the light and colours of the waterfall.

5. You might find it helpful to list and honour the person's good qualities, for instance:

    I acknowledge your light, your greatness, your pathway in this lifetime, and all your amazing qualities [list them].

6. Imagine the person you are forgiving smiling and happy, receiving everything they desire.

7. Finish by thanking the person (or event) for any lessons you have learned, or ways you have become stronger, as a result of the situation.

8. You are now ready to emerge from the waterfall knowing your energies are crystal clear. You have set yourself and the other person free.

Many people tell me that in some instances, forgiveness just isn't possible, as the hurt is too deep. In response, I tell them this story of how I learned about forgiveness.

MY STORY OF FORGIVENESS

Many years ago I felt incredibly hurt by the actions of my good friend Peter. I was furious with him, and felt with absolute certainty that I was in the right, yet I was the injured party. I didn't see any possibility for forgiveness, and I held on to some very strong emotions for many months.

Divine synchronicity sometimes lends a helping hand, and a while later I was in my local library and picked up a book about grieving.

While flicking through the book I found a chapter on forgiveness. It hadn't dawned on me until then that I could actually just forgive Peter and move on.

It took a while to completely forgive him and two things were very important in the process. Firstly, I said a powerful forgiveness statement:

> I forgive you for not being the person I wanted you to be — I forgive you and I set you free.

The second part was more difficult, which I'm sure you will understand if you have ever been furious with someone. I visualised Peter smiling and happy, receiving everything he wanted.

To be honest, in the beginning, I was only able to do this for a moment or two, and I may not have really meant it the first few times. It was difficult, but I persevered. On a soul level, I knew it was very important to forgive Peter. Gradually I was able to spend a little more time each day seeing him smiling and happy and I started to lighten up myself.

A few weeks later, I knew that I had completely forgiven Peter when I met him unexpectedly and didn't experience any negative emotions or expectations. I had cut the cords of anger between us. I even had a short, but pleasant, conversation with him! Ultimately, we were able to get past the negative event with forgiveness.

FORGIVING YOURSELF

Sometimes the person we need to forgive most of all is ourselves. This can be for mistakes we have made, things we have done or said, or for how we have treated ourselves. The previous exercise of the waterfall can be adapted for forgiving yourself. Simply replace the person or event with yourself, and say the forgiveness prayer:

> I forgive myself for [whatever event].
> I know I was doing the very best I could at the time.
> I forgive myself and I set myself free.

Let the cleansing waterfall wash away all the bad energies relating to the issue, while filling your aura with divine love. When you have followed all the steps, know that you are healed and your energies are crystal clear.

ASKING OTHERS TO FORGIVE YOU

Perhaps right now you need to ask someone else to forgive you. As relationships are complex and, usually, no one is totally to blame for something, you might find it helpful to do one of the previous exercises first; either forgiving yourself, or forgiving others, whichever is appropriate. Then, with an open heart, you will be able to ask for forgiveness.

Forgiving others makes it easier for the other person to respond with love, and helps create the bridge for them to forgive you. If this isn't the case, accept the person's decision with grace. Saying the forgiveness prayer at the end of this chapter will cut any cords and attachments between you, while accepting their decision will ensure that no further ones are formed.

Sometimes it isn't possible to directly ask a person for forgiveness, and the following prayer is also appropriate in this case.

> I ask for forgiveness from [person's name] for [whatever event].
> I ask for divine love and light to pour into this situation and dissolve the cords and hurt between us.
> Let us now go forth in love and light.

HAVE I FORGIVEN AND LET GO?

While writing this section of the book I realised there were many people and events that I thought I had let go of, but had never actually acknowledged or sent forgiveness to. So, I made a list of all those things and worked my way through it. The transformation and freedom I felt, as well as the insights I received, were amazing.

 Forgiveness has the potential to transform all to love, and is a gift you can give yourself and others.

FORGIVENESS PRAYER

You may also choose to say the following powerful forgiveness prayer. It calls forward a divine dispensation for any hurt or harm caused by ourselves or others.

Allow the healing light of forgiveness to shine from your heart as you say this prayer.

FORGIVENESS PRAYER

I forgive everyone who has ever hurt or harmed me,
through their thoughts, words or actions.
I know they were doing the very best they could at the time.
I now see them in their Divine perfection,
radiant with light and love.
I forgive them and I set them free.

I forgive myself for anything I have ever done
to hurt or harm myself and others
through my thoughts, words or actions.
I know I was doing the very best I could at the time.
I now see myself in my Divine perfection,
radiant with light and love.
I forgive myself and I set myself free.

I ask for forgiveness from anyone I have ever hurt or harmed
through my thoughts, words or actions.
I know I was doing the very best I could at the time.
I ask that Divine love and light pour into all situations
dissolving the cords and hurt between us.
I accept forgiveness and I set us all free.

Cutting cords

 Reclaim your vitality, freedom and power.

THE FORMATION OF CORDS AND ATTACHMENTS

Unresolved issues, old memories and emotional wounds—feelings of anger, hurt and neediness—all form cords to the issues or person involved, until they can be healed. They can create energy leaks—a flow of energy from us to another person or thing, draining us of our life force.

Cords create stress, which has a heavy energy, and can be like a ball and chain weighing us down. They are usually formed when we look outside ourselves for what we want, in the belief that only certain people or things can fulfil our needs. Or, we may want to keep something a certain way, which limits not only our freedom, but the freedom of others.

Sometimes other people send cords to us when they want us to meet their needs.

The shape and size of cords vary, depending on how long we have had the cords, and the strength of our emotion or desire. They can be like thick, heavy strands of energy extending out from our aura to someone else. Sometimes a person's aura may have many small cords, tiny strands of energy, formed as a result of worries, fears or expectations.

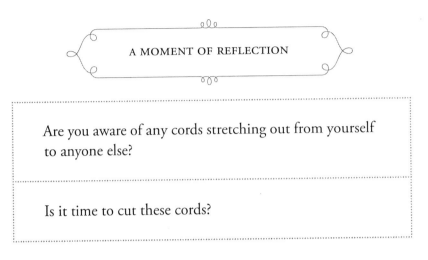

A MOMENT OF REFLECTION

Are you aware of any cords stretching out from yourself to anyone else?

Is it time to cut these cords?

CUTTING CORDS AND ATTACHMENTS

You can cut cords and reclaim your energy, setting yourself and others free.

The first steps in reclaiming your vitality, freedom and power, are taking responsibility for dealing with your issues, letting go of past hurts, and finding healthy and appropriate ways of meeting your needs.

STEPS FOR CUTTING CORDS

1. Focus on your energy field and, using your inner senses, see if you can feel whether you have any cords. Bring your attention inwards for a few moments to get an impression of their size and shape. Perhaps they are like lines of energy, or a heavy ball and chain. You may also get a sense of where the cords are attached between you and the other person, situation, or object.

2. Decide which cords you want to cut, focusing on only one or two cords at the same time.

3. Imagine a pair of golden scissors cutting the cords, and watch the lines of energy dissolve. Or, picture releasing the ball and

chain, the chain breaking open and setting you free.

4.   Send forgiveness, both to yourself and the other person. Forgiveness is a loving act which releases cords and attachments, literally letting the person 'off the hook'.

5.   Complete the process by focusing on the positive qualities and events you now want to create in your life.

6.   Celebrate your freedom!

CALL ON ARCHANGEL MICHAEL TO CUT CORDS

Archangel Michael helps to release negative energies from people, places or events. You can call upon Archangel Michael to cut away all cords and negative energy from you. He uses his great sword of truth to do this safely. If you ask, he will also place positive qualities in your aura, taking the place of the negativity that has been released.

MARIE'S STORY OF HEALING WITH ARCHANGEL MICHAEL

Marie asked Archangel Michael to assist her with a relationship that wasn't going well. She felt she needed to cut ties and clear her energy so that she could move on and stop feeling so drained.

Marie received very powerful healing as Archangel Michael filled her entire body and aura with a blue-white colour, and she was aware of the cords being cut easily. She also started to see the relationship and difficulties from a whole new perspective, which was very liberating.

The whole process took only ten minutes, and Marie was really amazed by how good she felt. Before this, a similar situation would have taken her weeks to work through and clear, but it was resolved by Archangel Michael with ease.

PREVENTING NEGATIVE CORDS AND ATTACHMENTS FORMING

At the end of the day, it is a good practice to review the day and let go of any concerns or worrying thoughts. Ask yourself, 'Does this issue need to be taken up again tomorrow, or has it served its time and purpose?'

Then cleanse your aura, forgive anyone who has hurt you, cut cords, and let go of any irritations. Be prepared to wake up in the morning bright and fresh, ready for a brand new day.

Cut cords, and set yourself and others free.

Disconnect from the collective consciousness

 I am the consciousness that dictates the course of my life. All outside influences, thoughts and beliefs fall away.

The collective consciousness contains significant negative ideas and thought forms which you may inadvertently take on board as your truth.

It is vital to understand this, as these 'truths' can have an enormous influence on your life — your thoughts and beliefs affect how you behave and create your reality. We all have an innate desire to be accepted and not be seen as different, so we are more likely to conform to what is regarded as the norm.

When you disconnect from the collective consciousness, you are free to make your own decisions. You can determine how you feel about the issues and events in your life.

THOUGHT FORMS WHICH INFLUENCE OUR LIVES

It is interesting to look at the major thought forms influencing us now, or those which have affected humanity in the past, causing turmoil and slowing down our spiritual growth.

At the moment, there is one large, prevalent thought form in the consciousness of humanity — the lack of abundance. This is causing incredible fear, worry, and hardship. When humanity as a whole refocuses on plenty and abundance, people will be more confident to spend money and finances will flow freely, benefitting everyone.

In the past, many major thought forms and beliefs were the cause of conflict and war. For instance, collective thoughts regarding people of different race and colour, or sexuality. Many of these collective thoughts and opinions are still affecting humanity today.

Anyone or anything that discriminates, or treats any life form as less than another, usually has roots in the beliefs of past generations of people.

It is time to transform the past and create an enlightened world.

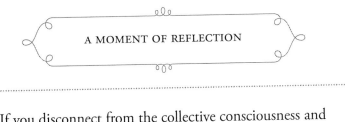

A MOMENT OF REFLECTION

If you disconnect from the collective consciousness and reclaim your freedom to decide your own thoughts, how could this change your beliefs and your life?

Is it time to cut these cords?

You step into your power when you are prepared to reassess your major thoughts, beliefs, and behaviours.

Cleansing with the Violet Flame

 Create miracles of love, joy and freedom in your life through the power of the Violet Light.

The Violet Flame is a powerful spiritual energy which accelerates our journey to enlightenment. It opens doorways to lightness, joy, love, and freedom. It cleanses, transforming negative thoughts, emotions or energy imbalances into the purity of light and love. It sets us free from all that holds us back.

People experience amazing results as they transform and lighten up through the power of the Flame. As it cleanses, it raises a person's vibration, bringing new lightness and vitality into their life.

St Germain is the guardian of the Violet Flame, along with Archangel Zadkiel and the Violet Flame Angels. There are many colours within the Violet Light, ranging from pink, blue and violet into amethyst and purple. Some people can actually 'see' the violet flames with their inner vision when they are working with the Flame.

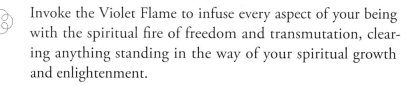 Invoke the Violet Flame to infuse every aspect of your being with the spiritual fire of freedom and transmutation, clearing anything standing in the way of your spiritual growth and enlightenment.

HELEN'S STORY: HOW THE VIOLET FLAME HEALS RELATIONSHIPS

Helen often felt small and dominated by her mother. As a result she felt resentful and angry, and she wanted to heal her relationship with her mother. Helen decided to invoke the Violet Flame to heal past hurts and traumas which had built up over the years. A lot of healing had already taken place, but she was aware that she still had some old patterns and behaviours affecting her relationship with her mother.

She was amazed at the power of the Flame. As she invoked it, she felt the Violet Flame surround her and layer by layer, old hurts and issues were cleansed. Helen was aware of the Violet Light working on her right to the core, transmuting the energy imprints of old wounds. Great burdens and clouds of negativity were released.

In her mind's eye she could see a clear white light of love forming between herself and her mother, where previously old, dark cords had joined them. She saw her mother as young and radiantly happy, and knew the work she had done on herself had also had a positive effect on her mother.

Helen felt a new lightness and maturity. Having let go of old child-hood issues, a door had opened, giving both herself and her mother the possibility of rekindling their relationship and becoming really good friends.

YOU CAN WORK WITH THE FLAME IN MANY WAYS

You can send it to:
- ◊ Cleanse negative emotions, old painful memories or hardened thoughts.
- ◊ Any physical ailment or disease. The Flame will enter every cell of your body, healing you. You can also send the Flame to help others who are unwell.
- ◊ Clear negative clouds of energy around events, people or places.
- ◊ Restore harmony in relationships.
- ◊ Heal past lives and dissolve bad karma, as well as ancestral and karmic bonds to others.

◊   Help heal the planet, dissolving the karma and pain of violence, injustice and war.

◊   Totally surround your aura when you are working through strong emotions such as fear or anger. While you are processing and resolving issues, your emotions will be contained within the Violet Light and not affect others, while healing yourself.

◊   Assist with issues you anticipate in your day ahead.

◊   Blaze a trail of light ahead of you each day, purifying all the places and situations you will encounter.

◊   Clear anything negative from your day by invoking the Violet Flame at night before going to sleep.

Working with the Violet Flame is a very simple yet powerful process. It can become part of your daily life.

SEVEN STEPS TO HELP YOU WORK WITH THE VIOLET FLAME

1.   Set aside time each day to do this work. Ten to fifteen minutes, preferably in the morning, or whenever you feel irritated or tired, is ideal.

2.   Ensure you are grounded. Visualise strong roots growing down into the ground from the soles of your feet, holding you solidly onto Mother Earth.

3.   Invoke protection. Visualise a golden white light of protection forming around your aura. You can also call on Archangel Michael's blue cloak of protection, a divine white light from Source, or the Gold Ray of Christ—they too will surround your aura and protect you.

4.   Start with a prayer. Invoke the Violet Flame, St Germain, Archangel Zadkiel and the Violet Flame Angels to work with you. Ask them to surround you with violet light.

5.   Visualise all the colours of the Violet Flame. See pink, blue, violet, amethyst and purple totally surround you. Watch it cleanse away the debris of negative thoughts, emotions, old patterns and imbalances. Feel it heal every organ in your body, and each layer of your aura.

6.   Send the Flame to a particular area or problem in your life, or invoke it to assist others.

7.   Visualise a bright white light forming in your auric field as lower energies are transformed and released.

8.   Thank St Germain and all the Angels for assisting you.

HEALING YOUR HEART WITH THE VIOLET FLAME

You can invoke the Violet Light to help you give and receive more love. It transforms the energies within your heart centre to liquid golden light. You can become aware of a new lightness and ease, along with deep compassion for everyone. This brings forgiveness and healing to relationships.

STEPS FOR HEALING YOUR HEART

1.   Allow yourself about fifteen to twenty minutes for this work. Take some time to get really comfortable and wrap yourself up warmly.

2.   Follow steps 2 to 3 in the exercise above to ensure you are grounded and protected.

3.   Invoke the Violet Flame, St Germain, Archangel Zadkiel and the Angels of the Violet Flame.

4. Start by sending the soft pink violet of the Flame to your heart and watch it flow throughout. It carries love, compassion and forgiveness for yourself and others. These are the qualities that heal the root of all disharmony.

5. See the pink violet flames radiating from your heart centre, like a pebble dropped in a lake, sending waves of pure love and forgiveness to every person, situation or thought form which has ever caused you hurt or pain.

6. Now call in all the violet rays of the Flame, including soft violet, amethyst and purple. See these flames transforming all the energy in and around your heart to the high frequency energy of liquid golden light. A new lightness, ease and joy bubbles up within you.

7. Liquid golden light now shines from your heart and forms a circle of golden light all around you. Now you can totally absorb its wonderful qualities of love, light and joy.

8. Visualise an oval light of protection around your aura again, or call on Archangel Michael to place his blue protective cloak around you. Ensure you are fully grounded.

9. Ask the Angels of the Violet Flame to continue to work with you throughout the day, and to help you stay centred in the loving energies of your heart.

10. Thank St Germain and all the Angels for assisting you on this healing journey.

VIOLET FLAME INVOCATIONS

Invocations are like prayers, calling on assistance or inspiration from a higher power. They are very powerful, and are best said slowly, with intent and love.

As you invoke the Flame, breathe in all its colours, from pink to amythest. See yourself surrounded by the Flame and then breathe in all its qualities—lightness, love, compassion, transformation, freedom, and joy.

INVOCATION FOR SPIRITUAL GROWTH AND ENLIGHTENMENT

I invoke the Violet Flame to infuse every aspect of my being with its spiritual fire of freedom and transmutation, clearing anything that stands in the way of my spiritual growth and enlightenment.

I ask my Angels, Guides, Saints and Ascended Masters, and the wisdom of my Higher Self, to oversee my transformation and guide me to my highest pathway.

INVOCATION FOR HEALING YOUR BODY

I ask the Violet Flame to flow into every electron, atom, molecule, cell, organ and system of my body, to cleanse and rejuvenate, allowing the divine blueprint of perfect health to manifest once more.

Take your time and visualise the Flame flowing throughout your whole body, focusing on any areas where you particularly want to receive healing. Hold a picture in your mind of each cell and organ lighting up with perfect health.

INVOCATION FOR RELEASING THOUGHTS AND WORRIES

I now release any old worries or thought forms about [insert subject] into the Violet Flame of transmutation, where they will be transformed into the Light.

I now replace these worries with thoughts of beauty, wholeness, love, joy, peace and gratitude.

I am grateful for the new peace and light in my life.

Picture the Violet Flame spiralling around your thoughts and worries, cleansing and dissolving them, and opening you to higher wisdom, where perfect solutions are born.

A PAUSE FOR REFLECTION

Are there any areas of your life that you would like to heal with the Violet Flame?

Try writing your own invocations, and see how powerful they are when infused with the energy of your heart.

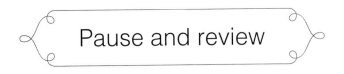

Pause and review

It is time to take another pause, and review your experience of working with the tools in this section.

 What areas of your growth and transformation are you particularly pleased with?

 Did you find the exercises on building confidence and stepping into your power helpful?

 Write down any of the changes you are planning to make in your life.

 Make a note of any insights or knowledge you received.

 Are there any areas of your life that you want to continue to focus on and transform?

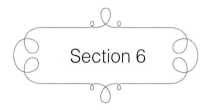

Section 6

Healing on all levels

There are many ways of healing all aspects of who you are.

This section contains information on the miracle of healing within your body, and various healing exercises you can do to heal on all levels. It explains how to clear unwanted thoughts, worries and fears, and provides guidelines on actively supporting your health and well-being.

A fifteen minute guided relaxation to refresh your mind, body and spirit is included with this book. See page vi for details.

Healing

....

A miracle of healing is constantly at work in your body.

THE MIRACLE OF HEALING WITHIN YOUR BODY

Your body always wants to heal itself and come back to balance. You can see this when you cut a finger. Your body starts a healing process that completely repairs the damaged tissue. It is the same with all tissues, organs and bones within your body.

To get an understanding of how healing works, it is important to understand that everything in existence is in a constant state of vibration, including every cell and system within your body. If an organ or system is out of balance, its rate of vibration (frequency) changes, and illness or disease may set in. An illness or symptom can be a signal that some part of your psyche is out of balance, and this is your body's way of bringing it to your attention for healing. Healing adjusts the rate of vibration of an organ or system and restores it to its natural, healthy frequency.

HEALING ON ALL LEVELS

◇ Energy blockages or lower frequency energies can cause illness or disease. At higher frequencies, these will no longer exist.
◇ Healing takes place when we raise our frequency to a higher level, where miracles are possible.
◇ A healer has the ability to connect a person to higher frequencies, channelling healing energies to them from the Angels, God, or the great cosmic pool of healing light. In doing so, they raise

that person's frequency, and remove any blockages.

◇ Many illnesses can fade away when we simply live with more love or joy in our hearts and deal with stresses or worries we have. Following the golden steps outlined in this book will help you not only on your path to enlightenment, but also to healing.

◇ You can support your body to heal by providing the right conditions for optimum health; through good nutrition, positive thoughts, reducing stress, and giving your body the time to rest and renew itself.

◇ If you have a health challenge, it is important not to judge yourself, as often our greatest learning comes from our challenges. Look instead to what you are learning and the many gifts your journey back to health and wholeness is offering.

SELF-HEALING EXERCISE

Unconditional love is the source of all healing. There is a constant source of divine healing energy available to you from God or Source, and within our multidimensional cosmos. You can also connect with the divine light within your heart and receive healing.

The Angels and Ascended Masters are always willing to assist you to heal—all you need do is ask.

STEPS FOR FLUSHING YOUR WHOLE BODY WITH HEALING LIGHT

1. Plan to spend about twenty minutes doing this exercise. To prepare, make sure that you are warm and comfortable—cover yourself with a blanket, as your body temperature may drop when you relax. You might like to light a candle and have relaxing music playing softly in the background.

2. Ask for healing light to flow to every cell and all that lies in between, flushing out any debris and stuck energy.

3. You may be aware of things clogging your cells—old thoughts, stagnant energies, perhaps even toxic substances and pollution.

4. Visualise those particles dissolving in the light, and all your cells becoming clear and bright. They shine with vibrant health, helping all parts of your body work perfectly. (Visualisation is a powerful process which harnesses the power of your mind, and supports your healing.)

5. Now ask the healing light to bathe all the layers of your aura, your thoughts and emotions, and the energies of your soul, in healing light.

6. If you wish, you can place your hands over your heart so that you energise them with loving energy from the divine spark within your heart. Then, place your hands on whatever part of your body you are working on, so that you focus the healing light there.

7. You may like to ask your Angels, Guides, Saints or Ascended Masters to also place their healing hands over yours, to increase the flow of divine, healing light.

8. Spend about ten to fifteen minutes bathing in healing light.

9. To finish, visualise an oval of protective white light forming around you, like the shell of an egg, enfolding you in loving energies.

HEALING IS A STEP-BY-STEP PROCESS

It is possible to receive instant healing. However, it usually happens at a pace that serves your highest good, in a balanced, gradual way, as part of a step-by-step process. To help yourself heal and rebalance, it is important to continue your step-by-step journey and do the healing exercises you feel particularly drawn to within the various sections of this book. Let your intuition guide you, and choose whatever exercise is most appropriate for you at a given time to heal on all levels — mind, body and spirit.

Above all, celebrate your successes and welcome the positive changes and new levels of lightness and well-being in your life.

Cleanse and refresh your aura

This is a wonderful exercise which will leave you feeling sparkling, energised and prepared for the day ahead. It will cleanse your aura on all levels, and light up every cell of your being with love, joy, and well-being.

The morning is the best time to do this exercise, as it sets you up for the day ahead.

STEPS FOR CLEANSING AND REFRESHING YOUR AURA

1. Imagine that you are standing under a sparkling waterfall of all the colours of the rainbow.

2. Visualise a sparkling rainbow stream of love, peace and joy flowing down through your physical body, dissolving stagnant energy, leaving you vibrant and fresh.

3. Then, visualise this sparkling stream flowing throughout your aura, cleansing any old emotions that may be holding you back.

4. Now see the sparkling stream grow wider, clearing away any old thoughts or worries that may have been bothering you.

5. The stream then flows throughout the spiritual layers of your aura, bringing lightness to every aspect of your being. Your aura is now a shining and radiant cloak of colour and light.

6. To finish, visualise a radiant golden light totally surrounding

the outside of your aura, like the shell of an egg, keeping your energies safe and protected.

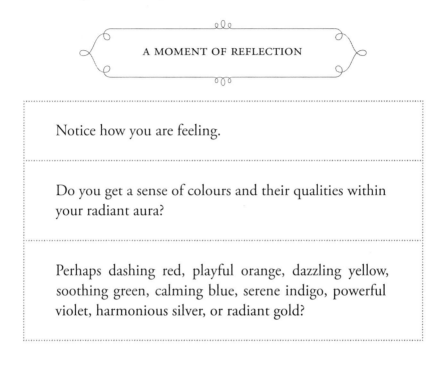

A MOMENT OF REFLECTION

Notice how you are feeling.

Do you get a sense of colours and their qualities within your radiant aura?

Perhaps dashing red, playful orange, dazzling yellow, soothing green, calming blue, serene indigo, powerful violet, harmonious silver, or radiant gold?

Self-care

On your journey to enlightenment, it is important to take care of your body—the vehicle for your soul's journey during this lifetime.

Taking care of your body and soul can be an enjoyable and life enhancing experience. In the sections which follow, simple steps are outlined, covering:
◊ Rest and relaxation.
◊ Correct breathing.
◊ Nourishment for body and soul.
◊ The benefits of exercise.

REST AND RELAXATION

It is in rest that the greatest work is done.

If you are constantly rushing around, striving to meet deadlines and expectations, you may accomplish many things, but miss out on the most important aspects of life.

There is no doubt about it; life has definitely got busier and time seems to have sped up. There are more financial pressures than ever before. With advances in technology, communication has the potential to be almost instantaneous, which places us under pressure to respond immediately.

Over the past three to five years, have you noticed whether your lifestyle and quality of life has changed? In all your busyness, do you allocate time for living joyfully, nurturing your relationships, and spending time in nature's beauty? These things will support your journey to enlightenment.

MESSAGES FROM YOUR BODY

Have you noticed that when you are feeling tired and stressed, it's also the time your back starts to ache or you get a headache? These are signals from your body that it is time to slow down or change what you are doing. What stress signals does your body give you?

It is so important to give yourself time to rest, relax, and recharge your batteries. When you have reserves of energy, you will find that you can cope better with life's demands, and actually accomplish more.

If you find yourself stressed and tired, take the time to listen to my fifteen minute guided relaxation, which will refresh your mind, body and spirit. See page vi for details.

SETTING PRIORITIES

With all the tasks we are asked to accomplish each day, it is easy to commit ourselves to far too much. The desire to do everything for everyone can leave us depleted. In this end, this only leaves ourselves and others short-changed.

The following things are crucial for your happiness and well-being: setting priorities, delegating, having clear boundaries, only taking on as much as you can cope with, and allocating time for rest and relaxation.

Do you feel selfish when you take time to rest or do what you want to do? Of course, balance is essential, but it is crucial to do what makes your heart sing. Remember, your joyful presence is one of the greatest gifts you can give to others.

CORRECT BREATHING

> Breath is the bridge which connects life to consciousness,
> which unites your body to your thoughts.
> —Thich Nhat Hanh

Our breath is a life-force energy, which nurtures both body and soul. In fact, in Latin, the word *spiritus* means both 'spirit' and 'breath'.

How many of us breathe correctly, so that we can bring this life-sustaining energy to every cell within our body? As we improve the quality of our breathing, we improve the quality of life-force energy available to us.

It is easy to learn how to breathe correctly. It only takes a small amount of practice each day, and soon becomes automatic. Two exercises are outlined below, first asking you to notice your breathing, and then if necessary, take steps to improve it.

NOTICING YOUR BREATHING

1. Stand with your spine straight and take a long slow deep breath. Breathe into your lower rib cage and stomach, and allow your stomach to expand like a balloon. This is breathing from your diaphragm, a band of muscle just below your rib cage. Breathing in this way allows the greatest amount of air to enter your lungs.

2. If you notice that your shoulders are rising as you breathe in and your rib cage isn't expanding, then you are breathing mostly into the top of your lungs. Your lungs are not filling up to their fullest capacity.

IMPROVING YOUR BREATHING

1. Lie down on the floor, relax and place your hands on your stomach.

2.   Now as you take a slow relaxed breath in, send the air all the way down to your stomach and notice that your hands are moving outwards as your stomach expands.

3.   Still breathing in, notice that your rib cage is expanding while you totally fill your lungs.

4.   As you slowly breathe out, your rib cage and stomach return to normal.

5.   Continue this cycle of breathing for a few minutes.

Breathing in this way feels very natural, and comfortable.

While you are developing a new habitual way of breathing, stop a couple of times during the day and notice how your lungs are expanding and if necessary, focus on breathing from your diaphragm again.

NOURISHMENT FOR BODY AND SOUL

A book of golden steps to inner peace, happiness and enlightenment wouldn't be complete without mentioning how our food supports our journey, as the food we eat builds our bodies, the sacred vehicle of our soul.

Just as your car wouldn't run well on contaminated petrol, it is important that you nurture yourself with the highest quality fresh food. As with everything in life, balance is important. A good, varied diet includes lots of vegetables, green salads, water, fresh juices and smoothies. All of these contribute to your good health. Keep the amount of processed foods, additives, preservatives and sugar to a minimum.

THE BENEFITS OF EXERCISE

We all know how important exercise is for our health and well-being. Rather than exercise being something that we 'have to do', it is much more fun to do activities that we enjoy. There are so many choices, for instance; walking, cycling, swimming, surfing, yoga … the list is endless. What would you like to try?

Choose whatever brings you the most joy. You may even decide to make it a hobby, and perhaps invite your friends to join you. Try combining your exercise programme with visits to beautiful places, so you nurture both your body and soul.

 Take care, and nourish yourself so you can feel good, look good and have more energy to enjoy life.

The power of thoughts

 Your thoughts hold one of the most important keys to inner peace, happiness and enlightenment.

A very wise teacher once told me that the two most important things in life are the thoughts we think and the food we eat. Your thoughts, originating from the centre of your consciousness, have a huge effect on all aspects of your life; physical, emotional, mental and spiritual.

Thoughts are powerful seeds of creation. Every thought you think sends out a little burst of energy. The stronger your feelings and thoughts, the more energy is transmitted. As your thoughts create your reality, it is so important to choose positive thoughts, and use the energy of your thoughts wisely to create happy and harmonious events all around you.

We can think up to 70,000 thoughts per day, perhaps more. It is quite possible that many of these thoughts are negative! We must work on turning our thoughts to positivity, and use them to serve our highest good.

 Let your mind be clear and bright, full of thoughts that serve your highest good and support your journey to enlightenment.

YOU CAN CHOOSE TO HOLD ENLIGHTENED THOUGHTS

You can create heaven in your life by letting every thought you think be clear, bright, and full of love, light, joy and harmony. You can choose the thoughts you think, thoughts that will serve your highest good and accelerate your journey to enlightenment. When your mind and thoughts are working well for you, your life flows smoothly so that you can live joyfully, full of love and light, and in touch with all the good of life.

It is important to understand that your mind will always be full of thoughts. Many people try to clear all thoughts from their mind, but that isn't possible—our minds are always working. However, you can decide what thoughts you want to give attention to. In effect, you can decide what to give your energy to, and what thoughts you want to fill your mind with.

Worry and negative thoughts are draining—they are like energy leaks, deflating your supply of energy and vitality—whereas happy thoughts are energising.

Whenever you find that you are thinking a negative thought or worrying, you can change it to positivity.

A MOMENT OF REFLECTION

Relax and focus on your thoughts for three minutes. Notice your thoughts, but don't judge or try to change them.

After three minutes, review what your mind was focused on.

Do your thoughts support and empower you? Are they infused with love?

TIPS FOR FOCUSING ON THE POSITIVE

◇ Start each day with a few minutes of positive thinking. Your focus on happy and loving thoughts will set you on course for the day.
◇ Spend a few minutes focusing on everything that is going well in your life, all the abundance, and everything that you are grateful for.
◇ Think happy thoughts and visualise success in everything you do.

When you focus on the positive, you are likely to be more relaxed and happy. You may also notice that you have more energy and vitality available for enjoying life.

 My thoughts nourish my soul and support my journey to enlightenment.

Clear mind chatter and circling thoughts

Our minds are constantly working, analysing and feeding information back to us about what is happening around us. This feedback helps to keep us safe, or to take action if needed.

However, if you find that your mind is full of unwanted thoughts, the following exercise will help clear the internal chatter and still your mind.

STEPS FOR CLEANSING YOUR MIND

1. Visualise white light pouring through your mind and brain, travelling along your neural pathways, clearing away old thoughts and debris, so that your mind is clear, fresh and open to new thoughts and ideas.

2. Do this for three to five minutes. If any distracting thoughts come into your mind, just gently bring your mind back to focus again on the cleansing white light.

ELEVATE ALL YOUR THOUGHTS TO THE HIGHEST LEVEL OF WISDOM

Elevating your thoughts to the highest level of wisdom is a key to enlightenment. By choosing to hold harmonious, loving, and peaceful thoughts, you connect to the higher aspects of your mind. Here you are more open to hear the wisdom of your intuition, the guidance from your Higher Self, and the promptings of your Angels and Guides.

HOW I CLEANSE MY MIND

Cleansing and refreshing my mind with white light is one of the most powerful exercises I do as part of my spiritual practice.

I flush my brain with white light and visualise it becoming radiant with the brightest light I can imagine. I see my mind merging with my higher mind and Higher Self and I know that I am connected to the light of my soul. In that moment I know that I am in control of my destiny and that my mind is flowing with a powerful and loving stream of high frequency light.

 Let your glorious mind be filled with thoughts of love, compassion and joy. Together we can bring heaven to earth, creating a beautiful world for everyone.

Worries, fears and negative emotions

TRANSFORMING WORRIES AND FEARS

Worries and fears can drain you of your life-force energy, joy and vitality. Have you ever felt like your whole mind was taken over by circling thoughts as you tried to find solutions to problems?

To bring an end to these draining thoughts, stop and remind yourself that you are much more than this worry or fear. You will be able to work through the issues, find solutions, and release whatever is upsetting you.

POINTERS FOR DISSOLVING WORRYING THOUGHTS AND FEARS

◇ It is always helpful to talk things through with a friend or counsellor. A problem shared is a problem halved.

◇ Watch your thoughts, and visualise everything working out perfectly, for the highest good of all. Support this with affirmations, for instance, 'Whatever is happening, I can cope, because _____.' Your positive attitude will bring you a new confidence in handling whatever comes your way.

◇ Visualise golden white light flowing throughout your mind and brain, dissolving your worries and fears.

◇ Call on your Angels, Guides, Saints or Ascended Masters to heal the source of the difficulty.

◇ Ask your Higher Self to guide you through the challenge and help you find the best solution.

DISSOLVING NEGATIVE EMOTIONS

If you are worried about something, your mind constantly whirring with anxiety, you are probably also feeling some unwanted, negative emotions. Emotional distress usually brings a message, and shows us which parts of our lives aren't working or serving our highest good. Have you experienced times when you felt overwhelmed with painful emotions, such as hurt, anger, jealousy, and betrayal? Have you doubted yourself? You may have felt like the spark had gone out of your life.

At such times, how can you find balance again and reconnect with the joy of life? There are many ways to do this so that you can move faster through the distress and challenges.

POINTERS FOR DEALING WITH NEGATIVE EMOTIONS

◇ It is really important to acknowledge your emotions and how you are feeling. Repressed or blocked emotions can clog up your system, making it more difficult to find solutions, or see the light at the end of the tunnel.

◇ Most of the negative emotions we experience involve other people. To heal distressing emotions and situations, it is helpful to imagine yourself and the other person surrounded by pink light, the colour of unconditional love. Imagine a bridge of love and light forming between you, where you can meet and sort out your difficulties.

◇ Talking things through with a friend or counsellor always help, acting like a pressure release valve, clearing some of the turmoil so you can see the situation from a new perspective.

◇ Having a good cry helps, as tears are your body's way of releasing stress, sadness, grief and anxiety.

◇ You can ask the Angels to help you dissolve the emotional blocks and tangles which are keeping you in turmoil.

◇ The thoughts you think create your emotions. Are you focusing on the positive, or are your thoughts adding to the turmoil? Try to keep your thoughts on all the good in your life.

◇ Cleanse your aura by imagining that you are standing under a waterfall, washing away the emotional debris.

 Let my mind be clear and bright and filled with thoughts that nourish me.

The present moment

 Rest into the stillness of the present moment, where you will find peace, love and joy.

We have already explored steps for stilling your mind and clearing circling thoughts. We will now look at the gift of the present moment, where stilling your mind and staying in the now frees up your energy, making it available to you.

THE GIFT OF THE PRESENT MOMENT

How often do you spend time worrying about things that happened in the past, or what might happen in the future?

 The present moment is where you can live your life to the full.

The present moment is all there is — the past is already past and the future has not yet arrived. It is in this present moment that you can experience all the joy, love and fulfilment that life has to offer.

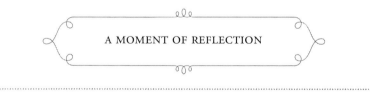

A MOMENT OF REFLECTION

Review the thoughts you have been giving attention to over the past five minutes.

Where have your thoughts been — in the past, worrying about the future, or centred in this present moment?

A short and useful exercise follows, which you can do whenever you find that your thoughts are straying to past or future events. You will bring your thoughts back to the present moment.

EXERCISE: LIVING IN THE PRESENT MOMENT

Start by closing your eyes. Breathe in and out.

◊ Breathe in peace and calm and breathe out any worries or concerns.

◊ Breathe in love and light and rest into the stillness you have created.

Repeat this cycle of breathing five times.

With each cycle, allow your breath and peaceful thoughts to relax you more and more, and bring you into the stillness of the present moment. Concerns about the future and past events fade away, and the gifts of the present moment — peace, love and joy — become available to you.

Cherish each precious moment. The past is in the past, the future has yet to arrive, but the present moment is a gift. It is a spark of light waiting for your attention, to lift your soul.

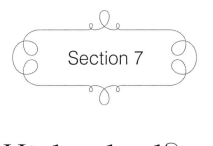

Section 7

Higher healing

Two powerful and transformative healing exercises are included in this section, both of which will help you heal and will hugely accelerate your spiritual growth and journey to enlightenment: the Oval of heavenly light and DNA Healing.

As both exercises are powerful and complex, I have written detailed instructions for you to follow so that you can gain the most benefit. It is also helpful to be guided through the whole process, so I have recorded both of these exercises for you to listen to. See page vi for details.

Please note: before doing these two powerful journeys, I highly recommend that you do the healing exercises outlined in the previous section first, as these exercises will provide the groundwork for the more in-depth, higher healing exercises which follow.

Oval of heavenly light

An experience of enlightenment

The healing exercise which follows is a gift from the Angels, Saints and Ascended Masters, so that you can receive deep healing, and expand your consciousness to such a level that you can experience an enlightened state of being.

It is very helpful to do this healing exercise, especially when you are feeling tired, depleted and in need of a boost. Creating an oval of heavenly light will help you step fully into your might and power, and know that you are a divine being of light.

The oval of heavenly light is a combination of:
◇   A matrix of high frequency divine light.
◇   Qualities of divine light and enlightenment—love, peace, appreciation, confidence, compassion, happiness and joy.
◇   Sparkling rainbow colours and sacred geometry.

While building your oval of heavenly light, you will:
◇   Merge with your Higher Self.
◇   Experience the essence of 'light' and enlightenment, as the Angels, Saints and Ascended Masters surround you with divine light.
◇   Receive deep healing throughout every aspect of who you are, your physical body, your thoughts and emotions.
◇   Your DNA will also be re-patterned with your perfect divine blueprint, so that every new cell created will hold a pure, heavenly light.

The oval of heavenly light forms a bubble of light all around you, extending out about a metre from your physical body.

HOW TO BUILD AN OVAL OF HEAVENLY LIGHT

This is a very sacred and powerful process. It is built in two parts:

1. Firstly, you must play your part in creating the energy around you, by choosing to surround yourself with many high frequency qualities and colours.

2. Your Higher Self, the Angels, Saints and Ascended Masters then fill the oval of light around you with the purity of divine light. This heavenly light can uplift your soul and expand your consciousness to such a level that you know that you are a divine being of light, perfect in every way.

STEPS FOR CREATING AN OVAL OF HEAVENLY LIGHT

1. *Preparation*
   Make sure you are comfortable and warm. Have a blanket nearby, as your body temperature may drop as you meditate and relax.

   You might like to light a candle, and play relaxing music softly in the background.

2. *Ground and protect yourself*
   Ensure that you are fully grounded by bringing your focus to your feet and sense or imagine that there are golden roots from your feet anchoring you solidly on the Earth.

   Ask for a golden ray from the heart of God or the cosmos to totally surround you in a bubble of radiant light. Alternatively, ask Archangel Michael, the great Archangel of Protection, to place his deep blue cloak of protection around you and ensure that only divine energies enter into your sacred environment.

3. *Relax and release stress and tension*
Focus on the rhythm of your breath, in and out, slowly and evenly. The gentle rhythm of your breath will help you relax, and release any stress or tension you may be holding.

4. *Fill your aura with a rainbow of colour and heavenly qualities*
Imagine a sparkling rainbow, full of colour and heavenly qualities, forming all around you, about a metre from your physical body. You can breathe in these heavenly qualities of love, peace, appreciation, confidence, compassion and joy.

Focus on each quality. Breathe it in to every cell and system of your body, and when you exhale, send it flowing out into your aura to surround you like a soft blanket, so that your aura becomes radiant with colour and light. Notice how you feel as you breathe in each quality and all the colours of the rainbow.

5. *Merge with the light of your Higher Self and receive deep healing*
Ask your Higher Self, the light of your soul, to merge with you and fill you with love, light and divine frequencies. Ask it to return you to the perfection of who are you, and to perfect balance and harmony on all levels.

A deep healing takes place as you merge with your Higher Self and shift to a higher frequency.

6. *The Angels, Saints and Ascended Masters surround you with heavenly light*
Ask the Angels, Saints and Ascended Masters to fill your aura

with divine frequencies, which build an oval of light all around you.

The light flows into every aspect of who you are, your physical body, your thoughts and emotions and the subtle energies of your spiritual bodies. Every cell and system is bathed in high frequency light.

Your DNA is being re-patterned with your perfect divine blueprint, and every new cell created within your body now holds a pure heavenly light.

The heavenly light contains many rainbow colours, and also colours that you may not be so familiar with — higher frequency pale, translucent or pearlescent colours, or colours tinged with silver and gold.

You may also be aware of geometric shapes and symbols forming around you. These are sacred geometric forms representing higher frequencies of light and consciousness. They may be moving, changing or merging with each other.

Bathe in this high frequency light, which uplifts your soul and expands your consciousness to such a level that you know that you are a divine being of light, perfect in every way — an enlightened being.

This is an experience of enlightenment.

Rest for a while and absorb this deeply healing and heavenly experience.

7. *Complete the journey and ground and protect yourself again*
   Ask the Angels, Saints and Ascended Masters to place a golden

white divine light all around you, surrounding your oval of light, so that you are totally held and protected in heavenly light.

Within this golden white light of protection, you will continue to hold the heavenly light and all the qualities you invoked—love, peace, appreciation, confidence, compassion and joy—close to you.

Thank your Higher Self and the Angels, Saints and Ascended Masters for the deep healing and experience of enlightenment you received, as they enfold you in heavenly light.

Bring your awareness back to the chair, bed or floor where you started this journey.

As you have been so open during this journey, ground yourself again by bringing your focus to your feet, and sense or imagine the golden roots from your feet anchoring you solidly on the Earth.

Finish by taking a few slightly deeper breaths, stretch gently, and open your eyes slowly.

Rest for a while to fully absorb all you have received.

MY OVAL OF HEAVENLY LIGHT

Creating my Oval of Heavenly Light was deeply healing and uplifting, and I experienced the oneness and interconnectedness within all of creation.

I was surrounded by a matrix of high frequency light and colour, and became one with this light, I knew that there was no separation. I was aware of the softness of the energy around me and felt total peace as small worries and concerns, were transformed, unable to exist in the presence of higher light. I was also aware of receiving guidance from my Higher Self, Angels, Saints and Ascended Masters, as wise thoughts dropped into my mind, showing me how to let go of minor tensions and concerns.

I felt deeply privileged and thankful for this sacred experience.

DNA healing

Cleanse and reprogramme your DNA with new life and energy.

Deep within the nucleus of every cell, your DNA contains your genes, which hold the divine design and blueprint for every cell, organ and system within your body.

Since the early 1950s when scientists first discovered this building block, we have been learning more and more about DNA.

Your DNA is similar to the programs on a computer, giving instructions for processes to be carried out. Like a computer in need of maintenance, you can remove the clutter of old programming and reboot your system, giving you a fresh new start.

BENEFITS OF DNA HEALING

Cleansing and reprogramming your DNA with new life and energy, and a new message of health, has many benefits.

◇ It gives you an opportunity to attain new levels of health and vitality, totally cleansed and emptied of pollutants on all levels—within your physical body, thought forms and emotions.
◇ You can release old patterns and memories so that you can have a fresh start, with freedom to choose new thoughts and patterns of behaviour.
◇ During the process of healing your DNA, you will communicate with the living consciousness within your body.
◇ You can send your body a new message of health and wholeness,

particularly if the codes within your genes render you susceptible to a particular illness, or if an organ or system within your
body is in need of healing.

◇   Above all, reprogramming your DNA gives you an opportunity
to hold the perfect, divine blueprint for all your cells, organs
and systems.

HEAL YOUR DNA

Healing your DNA is a very detailed, powerful and sacred process,
and is carried out in three parts. These are summarised below, and
the whole process is then explained in detail.

PART ONE

— Prepare for the healing you are about to receive.
You will ensure that you are grounded, invoke the assistance of
your Higher Self, Angels, Saints and Ascended Masters, and
request Archangel Michael to protect you in his blue cloak
of light.

PART TWO

— Request divine healing light to flush your DNA with new
life and energy.
As pure white divine healing light flows into the heart of your
DNA, it will flush your cells with its purity, and cleanse and
dissolve all blockages, stresses and pollutants, bringing new life
and energy to every cell.

PART THREE

— Reprogramme your DNA with a new message of health.
You will focus on the DNA within one cell of an organ or system
and request divine healing light to flow into the nucleus of that
cell, assisting it to return to its divine, perfect form.

Each cell is unique and complete within itself, and holds the design and blueprint for every other cell within an organ. As the individual cells communicate with every other cell, you can request that the healed cell send its new programme or message of health to all cells of that organ.

STEP-BY-STEP HEALING

Healing DNA is usually a step-by-step process, and will always happen in a balanced way, at a pace most suitable for you.

If dealing with a health issue which has built up over time, you may find it helpful to do this exercise a few times. It is an incredibly powerful healing treatment and its effectiveness increases with practice—be guided by your intuition.

GENETIC INHERITANCE AND SUSCEPTIBILITY TO CERTAIN ILLNESSES

If the codes within your genes render you susceptible to a certain illness, you may be calling forward a major learning experience in this lifetime, in accordance with your soul's decision, or the divine plan.

You can, however, ask for healing, if this is in line with your soul's plan and for your highest good.

When requesting healing, always ask your Higher Self to guide the healing. Perhaps you have already learned what you need from this particular illness or experience, and ask that anything else you need to do to support your healing be made clear to you.

STEPS FOR HEALING YOUR DNA

PART ONE

1. *Preparation*

    Make sure you are warm and comfortable. Wrap a blanket around yourself, as your body temperature may drop when you meditate and relax.

    You might like to light a candle or play relaxing music softly in the background.

2. *Ground yourself*

    Ensure that you are fully grounded by bringing your focus to your feet and sensing or imagining there are golden roots from your feet anchoring you solidly on the Earth.

3. *Invite your Higher Self, Angels, Saints and Ascended Masters to assist you*

    As your DNA expresses the consciousness of who you are, it is always helpful to invoke the assistance of your Higher Self and beings of light from the spiritual realms.

    You can also ask Archangel Michael, the great Archangel of Protection, to place his deep blue cloak of protection around you to ensure only divine energies enter into your sacred environment.

4. *Relax and release stress and tension*

    Close your eyes and focus on the rhythm of your breath. Breathe in and out, slowly and evenly. The gentle rhythm of your breathing will help you relax and release any stress or tension you may be holding.

PART TWO

5. *Request divine healing light from the heart of God or the cosmos to flush your DNA with new life and energy*

Sense or see white divine healing light flowing into the heart of your DNA, flushing your cells with its purity.

As it cleanses and dissolves blockages and all negative, stuck energy formed as a result of negative thinking, patterns of behaviour, poor diet, pollution, or stress, is released. This leaves space for fresh new energy to enter, bringing a sense of vitality.

At this stage, you have reached an incredible state of purity and clarity where it is possible to think clear and empowering thoughts. Your energy levels support you to do what you wish with your life, and your radiance creates peace and harmony all around you.

PART THREE

6. *Send healing to a particular organ or system and reprogramme your DNA with a new message of health*
Focus on the DNA within the nucleus of one cell of an organ or system, and call on divine healing light to flow into the nucleus of that cell.

As this is a very sacred and powerful process, ask your Higher Self, Angels, Saints and Ascended Masters to assist in reprogramming the DNA within this cell, so that it holds the perfect, divine blueprint for your health. Ask it to be done in accordance with the decision of your soul and the divine plan for your life.

Sense or see this special cell sparkling with radiant light, health and vitality.

This cell now sends the light of the new design and blueprint radiating out to all other cells within the organ.

Continue to rest for another five to ten minutes, while focusing on an image of light and health spreading from cell to cell, until all the cells within the organ are fresh and clear, radiant with light.

7.   *Complete the journey and ground and protect yourself again*
     Bring your awareness back to the chair, bed or floor where you started this journey.

     Ensure that you are grounded again by bringing your focus to your feet, and sense or imagine the golden roots from your feet anchoring you solidly on the Earth.

     Ask the beings of light from the spiritual realms to surround your body and aura with a golden white protective light.

     Thank your Higher Self and all the beings of light who have assisted you.

     Finish by taking a few slightly deeper breaths, stretch gently, and open your eyes slowly.

     Rest for a while to fully absorb all you have received.

A FRESH START AS YOU EMPTY AND REBOOT YOUR SYSTEM

Your DNA has now been upgraded with new instructions, similar to an upgrade to programs on a computer. As such, it is important to try not to think the same old thoughts, or focus on old issues and worries. Also, be mindful of any pollutants you may be taking into your body, which may affect your DNA.

You can decide what programmes (thoughts) to run, and what maintenance your system needs to keep it fresh and vibrant. Try to keep your energy as clear as possible by watching your thoughts, taking care of your diet, drinking plenty of clean water, and spending as much time as possible in the fresh energies of nature. Aim to have balance in your life, with plenty of time to relax and recharge your batteries.

 Live with awareness, and give yourself the gift of a fresh new start.

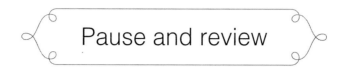

Pause and review

Review your experience of working with the healing exercises in sections 6 and 7.

 Which healing exercises were you particularly drawn to?

 Have you noticed any differences in your health? (Consider all levels — mind, body and spirit.)

Healing is usually an ongoing process requiring us to change some aspects of our lives and make healthy choices. Are you planning any changes?

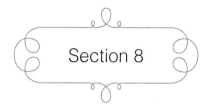

Section 8

The healing gifts
of nature

Mother Nature gives us many gifts which help us to open our hearts and find more peace, joy and harmony in our lives. These are the qualities that assist us on our journey to enlightenment.

Most of this book was inspired by and written in the beauty of nature, and I hope that in the following pages I can share some of that beauty and inspiration with you.

The healing gifts of nature

 Let the beauty of nature uplift your soul and support your journey to enlightenment.

SPENDING TIME IN NATURE OPENS OUR HEARTS

The beauty and purity of nature uplifts and inspires us, opens our hearts, and supports our healing and journey to enlightenment. When we spend time in nature, admiring the beauty all around us, our loving thoughts and appreciation fill our hearts with joy.

You might like to take a stroll in a beautiful place and admire and appreciate the gifts that Mother Nature gives us:

◇   The majestic hills and mountains, some snow-capped, with radiant auras of light.

◇   All the waters of the world, our magnificent oceans, rivers and lakes.

◇   Our forests and green meadows, the abundance of flowers in all the colours of the rainbow.

◇   The plentiful food provided for us, radiant with nourishment.

◇   The great diversity of life on our planet, all the animals, birds, fish and smaller creatures.

◇   Our beautiful planet that is our home and the home of our fellow human beings of many nationalities, cultures and beliefs, all on our journey home to the Light.

Thank you Mother Earth for the many gifts you give us—your beauty bathes our souls in peace and love.

HEALING IS NATURE'S GIFT TO US

 Mother Nature gives us many gifts to support our healing and enhance our well-being.

She shares her pristine clear energies with us, along with her many healing sounds and colours, and the healing gifts offered by all the elements — earth, air, water and fire.

NATURE'S LULLABY

The sounds of nature produce a relaxing lullaby, which uplifts our soul.

You can give yourself the gift of being soothed by nature's lullaby. Go somewhere as far away from man-made noise as possible and listen to:
- ◇ The breeze whispering through the leaves of trees.
- ◇ The lullaby of the ocean as its waves lap the shore.
- ◇ Cascading sounds of waterfalls and flowing rivers.
- ◇ The songs of the birds.
- ◇ The sounds of many animals.
- ◇ The myriad sounds all around you.

Close your eyes, listen, and allow the sounds of nature to uplift your soul and enhance your sense of well-being.

A RAINBOW OF COLOUR

Mother Nature offers us the gifts of her rainbow colours, each with different qualities, which nurture and energise us on all levels.

Breathe in the colours and their wonderful qualities into your body and aura, so you are surrounded by a rainbow cloak of light. Breathe in energising red, joyful orange, exciting yellow, harmonious green, calming blue, serene indigo and powerful violet.

The sounds and colours of nature nurture our soul, and help us rebalance and heal.

THE HEALING GIFTS OF THE FOUR ELEMENTS

All the elements of nature support our healing through their cleansing and energising effects.

You may wish to work with one of the elements, or create a ritual where you work with all four. If possible, go to a peaceful and beautiful place, where you are surrounded by all the elements of nature (with the exception of fire, of course).

EARTH

Place your feet firmly on Mother Earth and ground yourself. Imagine golden roots going down from the soles of your feet into the Earth. Mother Earth is willing to absorb any of your energies that are out of harmony, your thoughts or worries, and transform them into light. Imagine old energies flowing down through the soles of your feet into the Earth and being transformed.

When you connect to our Earth Mother's energy, you can receive all the nutrients you need. With your feet placed solidly on the Earth, imagine that all the good in life and all the nutrients and energies this planet offers are flowing to you through the soles of your feet.

AIR

A blustery day is uplifting and invigorating. The breeze will cleanse your aura, as it blows away old energies, thoughts and emotions.

Breathe clear air into your lungs. It will be carried to every cell and system, bringing freshness and vitality.

WATER

Imagine that you are standing under a waterfall or swimming in the ocean. The fountain of water or waves will wash away any debris, cleansing your aura. Imagine the water flowing through your veins, in between your cells, and all through your body, flushing out impurities.

As our bodies are approximately 70% water, it is helpful to drink a glass of pure water mindfully, hydrating your entire being.

FIRE

Fire transforms and cleanses, making room for the new to come in and flourish. Imagine putting old issues, thoughts, even your old clothes and possessions, in a bonfire. Afterwards, notice that you now have new clothes and possessions nearby. Thank Mother Nature for the abundance and transformation she brings.

Once you have worked with your element, finish by thanking Mother Nature and all the elements for the gifts you have received.

Love and kindness for animals

 Celebrate each life form. Appreciate their uniqueness and special contribution to life on our planet.

This section is dedicated to my treasured dog Skippy, now passed on to spirit, for the love, companionship and wonderful walks in nature which she shared with me for thirteen years. I'm grateful to her for her quiet presence as she sat behind me on my chair while I typed my work. Also to the new arrival—Bella, the black beauty—a loving collie dog with boundless energy, who likes to cuddle up close.

LOVE FOR ANIMALS IS A QUALITY OF ENLIGHTENMENT

We share our planet with a great diversity of life. Animals have an abundance of love to share and so much to teach us. They have their own soul and purpose for being here, and are learning and growing just as we are.

When we understand the oneness within all of creation, that we are all connected, it is a natural step to live in a way that honours every life form. This is an important step in our evolution, as we create a beautiful new world together, while opening a doorway to enlightenment.

EVOLVING AND SEEING WITH NEW EYES

At different times in our lives, as we change and grow, we are called on to look at things differently and to see with 'new' eyes. As humanity has grown and evolved throughout the ages, we have taken many giant leaps in our evolution.

Our journey to enlightenment now asks us to take another major leap forward, and see with new eyes that all life forms are unique, special gifts of creation.

MY STORY: THE EYES OF A GREAT HUMPBACK WHALE

It is an awesome experience to look into the eyes of a whale—you can see the deep wisdom and gentleness of its soul.

In 2007 I had an opportunity to swim with humpback whales in the Silver Banks, a protected sanctuary in the ocean, eighty miles from the Dominican Republic. Whales come there every year to give birth and stay for three or four months to nurture their young in safety.

During the week we were there, our home was a small live-aboard boat. Everything was done with the utmost respect for the whales and their environment.

Each day we got into a smaller boat and stopped close to where we could see the whales sending up spouts of air through their blow-holes. We then telepathically asked their permission to enter the water. If the answer was yes, we slipped in quietly and respectfully, in the hope of being close to them in their home, the ocean.

On one of these special days I received a very profound and life-altering message which I wasn't expecting. A mother and baby were nearby, and we accepted their invitation to swim close to them.

As we slowly swam towards the mother and calf, I looked into the eyes of the mother whale—so soft, gentle and deep. The eyes are windows to the soul. She told me that it was fine to look into her eyes, but that I should start spreading a message to others, asking them to look into the eyes of every creature and see how unique and special they are.

The welfare of animals is a topic very close to my heart, and this profound message from a great humpback whale moved me to tears. It gave me renewed energy and fuelled my enthusiasm to follow her advice and look for ways to help people see the uniqueness and specialness within all life forms.

THE EYES ARE WINDOWS TO THE SOUL

It is amazing to look into the eyes of animals. You form a deep connection with them and see the essence of who they truly are. You have probably done this many times with your own special pet and have seen a wonderful creature looking back at you, so full of pure unconditional love.

It is a very profound experience to also look into the eyes of other animals, for instance farm animals. Have you ever looked deep into the eyes of a cow to really see the essence of this gentle creature? Or other animals such as horses, sheep or pigs?

When you approach an animal with love and look into its eyes with the intention of connecting and understanding who the animal is, you will feel a connection in your heart. It is a deep feeling of compassion and love. Don't be surprised if you also feel you are communicating with the animal. When you look deeply into its eyes with an open heart and mind, you can sense its essence, and you also open a channel of communication.

SEE ALL LIFE ON THIS PLANET THROUGH NEW EYES

The exercise which follows is good fun. It asks you to go for a walk and imagine that you are visiting Earth from a distant planet, and this is your first day here. Everything you see and do is new and exciting.

For this exercise, all you need is an open heart and mind.

1. Can you imagine arriving on this planet and seeing everything for the first time? Perhaps you are a visitor from a distant planet and have just arrived for a new adventure.

2. Go for a slow stroll in the local park or countryside.

3. As you walk, look around. There is a huge variety of life forms here, some tall with two legs, and others furry with four legs. Some life forms spend most of their time off the ground and have wings, and there are lots of tiny creatures with many legs. They all seem to enjoy doing different things and all contribute something special to the planet.

4. If you have the opportunity, gently approach some of the life forms and mentally ask if it is OK to look into their eyes. Send love as you do this, and as you look into each animal's eyes you will get a sense of their essence and energy.

5. You might also like to talk to the animals or ask a question.

6. Enjoy your walk and the excitement of seeing everything for the first time as you look around with new eyes.

When we open our hearts and minds to our fellow creatures, we open ourselves to even greater levels of love—one of the main qualities of enlightenment.

ANIMALS COME INTO OUR LIVES TO SUPPORT US

Animals have their own special life mission and tasks while here on Earth. Often, their task is to assist us. For instance, dogs and cats help to open hearts, bees teach us about organisation and working together, and cows teach us about gentleness. If we open our eyes we can see their special qualities and learn from them.

Dogs, cats and other special pets particularly teach us about unconditional love. They just want to love us and be loved in return.

As our journey to enlightenment is an open-hearted journey of love, animals have a very important role to play.

STORY: A SPECIAL DOG CALLED ANGEL WHO HELPED OPEN HEARTS

In 2010 I went on a spiritual journey to a retreat centre in Brazil to visit John of God, who has special healing abilities. While out walking with two friends, we found a little puppy who had made its home in some long grass beside a track, just up the hill from the centre. Someone had obviously dumped it there in the hope that a kind person attending the healing retreat would give it a home.

The little puppy would run into the grass every time someone approached, defending its territory with a few puppy growls and barks. That's not very good behaviour when you need someone to bring you food, or take you home.

We were concerned about the puppy because it was thin and we didn't want it to go hungry. So we started to bring it food. At first we had to leave the food by the side of the track and move away, as the puppy would hide in the grass until it felt it was safe to come out. Then after a few days it started to trust us, and would run out excitedly whenever we appeared.

We called the little dog Angel because she was so special. Everyone who saw Angel fell in love with her.

As we were only staying for two weeks, and really wanted to find a home for Angel before we left, we asked the Angels of Animals to help us find a perfect home for our little dog.

Then with divine synchronicity, we met some wonderful people who were very willing to help. On the last evening we met Rory, a lovely Irish man, who was delighted to keep feeding Angel until she found her new home. We later heard that Angel had been adopted by a friend of Rory's, who was taking good care of her.

The healing retreat with John of God was based on love, and our little Angel played a special role in opening many hearts.

MY DOG SKIPPY CAME INTO MY LIFE IN A VERY SPECIAL WAY

I was driving along a narrow country road when a little rascal of a dog ran in front of my car. Thankfully, I was driving slowly and managed to avoid her, and the car behind me also had a near miss. I stopped to see why this little thing was out in the middle of nowhere, throwing herself in front of cars and having close escapes.

She was a very thin little dog, barely more than a puppy, and it looked like someone had abandoned her. So I put her in the car and spent the morning calling to various animal rescue centres to see if they could take her in. The centres I called to always find a place for a lost animal, but this particular morning no one had room. I think I now know why this happened — they quickly saw that I was already smitten with this little creature and knew she would be OK, leaving a place free for another dog. So, I opened my heart and home to the rascal that was by now 'my dog'.

Throughout her life, Skippy continued to weave her magic, making people laugh with her funny antics, and loved people with incredible enthusiasm. She had a knack of bringing people together, and her loving presence opened many hearts and healed relationships.

After thirteen years of fun and love, Skippy passed into the world of spirit. I still feel her gentle presence around me, particularly when I am driving or walking in the hills. She is always in my heart, just a thought away.

You probably have your own story about an amazing animal in your life.

COMMUNICATING WITH ANIMALS

We can all communicate with animals. Animals speak to us, just in a different language. We can hear their messages telepathically as thoughts or images in our mind, or intuitively through the feelings they convey. We can also telepathically talk to animals and be understood, or ask a question and receive a reply.

Telepathic communication is a stream of thoughts or consciousness which you send from your mind to someone else. We are all telepathic, and can send and receive information. I'm sure you have experienced times when you knew what a person was going to say before they said it, or who was at your front door before they even rang the bell.

Now, more and more people are recognising that it is possible to hear the language of animals. Just like any skill, it takes a little time and practice.

Perhaps you would like to try the following exercise and communicate with a special animal in your life.

Start first of all with your own pet, as you already have a close bond. (If you don't have a pet of your own, perhaps you can try to communicate with a friend's pet.)

If you can, do this exercise with your pet by your side. If this isn't possible, hold a photograph of it, or keep an image of your pet in your mind.

1. Find a quiet place where you won't be disturbed. Focus on your breathing as you settle down and relax.

2. Close your eyes and imagine that you are surrounded by a soft pink blanket of love. Breathe this soft pink colour into your heart with the intention of opening it even more.

3. Now send this soft pink colour of love to your pet. In your mind's eye picture your pet surrounded by a bubble of love, with both of you connected by the pink light.

4. If your pet is with you, mentally tell it that you would like to communicate with it. (If you are holding a picture or an image of your animal in your mind, you can also telepathically tell the animal that you would like to communicate with it.)

5. Talk to your pet and ask a question if you wish. To receive a reply, just listen with an open mind and you will find thoughts or images dropping into your mind.

6. You can ask your pet if there is anything it would like to tell you. Again listen with an open mind and you will be amazed by the information you receive.

7. Finish by sending your pet lots of love and thanks.

SUE'S IRISH WOLFHOUND

My friend Sue has a lovely Irish wolfhound whom she loves dearly. His name, Blue, comes from the silvery-blue colour of his coat. They live in the countryside where there are many farms and sheep. Blue loves to run through the fields, and for a time Sue was worried that the local farmers might think he was too close to the fields where they kept their sheep.

It was difficult to stop Blue from running, and Sue had to confine him to a small part of their yard for a few months. Sue knew that it was possible to talk to animals, but she hadn't done it before. After taking part in a course on communicating with animals, Sue went home, sat down with Blue and talked to him. She told him about the dangers of running in fields near sheep, and asked him not to go running anywhere beyond their own land.

That was all that was needed—Sue only had to ask once. From then on, he still enjoyed running, but stayed safely within the boundaries of their own fields.

COMMUNICATING WITH ANIMALS THAT HAVE DIED

We can also communicate with pets that have died. They will often stay around us, continuing to love and protect us.

MARGARET'S TERRIER

Margaret often felt sad and puzzled because her little terrier dog Russ died suddenly, when no one was around. She felt a little guilty, as she would have brought Russ to the vet had she known he was unwell, and perhaps he would have lived for a few more years.

The first time Margaret took part in an animal communication exercise, she immediately connected with Russ and was surprised by how easy it was to talk to him. He was delighted to make contact, and told her that a few days before he died, he had been hit by a car when the family was out. Russ also told Margaret not to feel bad about what had happened, as he was very happy in the spirit world and often visited the family.

This was a very profound experience for Margaret, and she felt hugely relieved to know that Russ was happy and often close by.

To communicate with an animal that has died, follow the steps of the previous exercise on communication, while holding a picture of your pet, or an image of your pet in your mind.

COMMUNICATING WITH OTHER ANIMALS

As well as communicating with our pets, it is very interesting to communicate with other animals, for instance farm animals, wildlife such as lions or monkeys, or even animals you don't particularly like. You can talk to them and ask them what their purpose is here on Earth. The answer is always interesting and illuminating.

If you would like support as you learn this new skill, you will find there are many courses in animal communication out there to choose from.

LIVING IN HARMONY WITH ALL ANIMALS

It is my deepest wish that we start to treat all animals, particularly our farm animals, in a new and compassionate way.

We were once taught that humanity was the top form of life on the planet and had dominion over all other creatures. Now that we are taking a giant leap forward in our evolution, we are being called to see and do things differently.

We are answering this call in many ways. There is a growing movement away from the fast-food and intense farming methods which have become the norm over the past fifty years, in favour of organic and vegetarian produce. More and more people who eat meat now also want to know how the animals were kept, if they were free to roam outside in the fields, and if they were treated with respect. In fact, many people find that as they live with awareness, they no longer want to eat meat. Instead they are drawn to a vegetarian diet, full of freshness and nutrients.

People want to know that the products they buy have been produced without carrying out painful tests on animals. Not only this, but in most parts of the world, attitudes towards wearing fur coats (and other fur clothing) have changed so much that they are no longer fashion items.

Now that we are learning to communicate with animals, it would be wonderful if we asked our fellow creatures a few simple questions, for instance, 'What do you need for your comfort?' or 'Are you happy in this field?' This could be something you would like to try.

 Our journey to enlightenment is an open-hearted one. Let us make a commitment to love, honour and respect, and live in harmony with the great diversity of life on this planet.

Dolphins—the angels of the ocean

Dolphins radiate a high frequency light. As they enfold us in their essence of love, joy and bliss, they help us anchor these wonderful qualities in our lives, accelerating our journey to enlightenment.

Dolphins play a special role in our lives, and this book wouldn't be complete without mentioning them. They are known as the Angels of the Ocean, and radiate love, joy and bliss. You can connect with dolphins either in meditation, or by visiting them as they swim freely in the ocean.

Swimming with dolphins is a magical experience. Many people are drawn towards dolphins, as they can sense that there is something special about them.

DOLPHINS ASSIST US ON OUR JOURNEY TO ENLIGHTENMENT

All dolphins are healers. They enfold everyone in their presence with their vibrant auras of light and joy, and reconnect people with their own essence of love, happiness and well-being. Healing then takes place on many levels.

As the love and joy of the dolphins touches our hearts, we expand effortlessly into the fullness of who we are. I have seen this happen so many times as people visit dolphins by boat, or swim and play with them in the ocean. They feel a sense of happiness and peace, and a touch of Heaven on Earth is created.

191

SWIMMING WITH DOLPHINS

I have been blessed with the joy and privilege of swimming with dolphins in the warm oceans around Hawaii and the Bahamas, and also with some very special dolphins in the Atlantic Ocean off the west coast of Ireland.

It is a magical experience, and it has helped me stay in touch with my own inner essence of love and joy. Dolphins give us a special gift by reminding us of who we truly are. They give us a taste of what life could be like as we evolve and move forward on our journey to enlightenment.

Note: If you are planning a trip to meet the dolphins, please plan to see them in their natural environment as they freely swim in the ocean. Many companies in various parts of the world offer boat trips in a respectful way that honours the freedom of the dolphins.

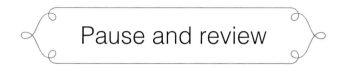

Pause and review

 Have you taken the time to explore the many healing gifts of Nature?

 Make a note of any insights or new information you received.

 What was your best experience?

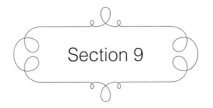

You can light up
the world

So far you have focused on your own journey to inner peace, hap-piness and enlightenment, through healing, transformation, and lighting up your life with golden opportunities.

Are you now ready to take the journey a step further, and take on the important role of Ambassador for the Light, spreading peace, love and harmony all around you? Are you willing to help create Heaven on Earth?

An Ambassador for the Light

 I offer myself as an Ambassador for the Light, to spread love, light, peace and harmony all around me.

Offering to be an Ambassador for the Light is a great service for mankind. You will be a beacon of light, transforming lower energies and showing others the way.

HOW TO PREPARE TO BE AN AMBASSADOR FOR THE LIGHT

1. Declare your intention to be an Ambassador for the Light, to spread love, light, peace and harmony all around you, through all you do.

2. Keep your aura clear and bright by spending time in nature, having a daily spiritual practice, including prayer or meditation, and ensuring your thoughts and actions are infused with love.

3. Each day, affirm or remind yourself that you are a divine being, radiant with light and love. Knowing who you truly are allows your light to become even more radiant, and brings about many changes which will transform your life so that you can fully step into the important role of Ambassador for the Light.

YOUR RESPONSIBILITIES AS AN AMBASSADOR FOR THE LIGHT

1. Always aim to see the divinity and potential within each person and in all life forms.

2.   Speak only words of encouragement to everyone, whatever their circumstances.

3.   See every person surrounded by love and light, and hold the vision of them achieving their heart's desire.

4.   Offer support in whatever way is appropriate, either through giving direct assistance, enfolding the person or situation in healing light, or perhaps offering another viewpoint infused with the highest perspective.

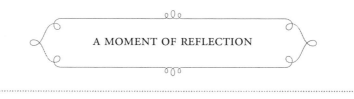

A MOMENT OF REFLECTION

As an Ambassador for the Light, is there any service work that you would particularly like to offer, or project you would like to support?

A TEAM TO SUPPORT YOU

You will be supported in your work by many great beings of light from the spiritual realms—your Angels, Archangels, Guides, Saints and Ascended Masters. When you declare your intention to be an Ambassador for the Light, your intention is noted and many divine beings come forward to support you.

I am here to represent Him who sent me.
—from *A Course in Miracles*

Creating Heaven on Earth

Be the change you want to see in the world.
— Mahatma Gandhi

As an Ambassador for the Light, you can assist with creating Heaven on Earth.

WHAT DOES CREATING HEAVEN ON EARTH MEAN?

Remember the many times when your heart has been wide open and you have felt joyful, loving life, and overflowing with love and compassion for everyone. You may have felt your life was touched by 'Heaven', everything harmonious and full of possibilities. This is the essence of Heaven on Earth.

Bringing Heaven to Earth involves creating a world you would like to live in — where people live their lives based on love, joy, peace, abundance, harmony and fulfilment — all the qualities of enlightenment.

Our world is in transition at the moment as we move from the world we have known for a very long time, to a bright new golden world, where we live as enlightened beings of love and peace, creating harmony all around us.

THE RIPPLE EFFECT — CREATING HEAVEN ON EARTH

You have a role to play in the creation of a beautiful world, as every act of love, every thought and action, has an effect.

Everything is interconnected, and everyone's contribution is important. As each of us experiences more love, joy and peace in our own lives, we create a wave of light which radiates out from us, transforming all to love.

As your loving, joyful and peaceful presence uplifts everyone around you, those people in turn will radiate their light and love to everyone around them. These waves of love spread so a worldwide ripple effect is generated, giving us the possibility of creating Heaven on Earth.

   Your presence makes a big difference in the world.

Golden communities

Golden communities are built with a golden energy, and all the qualities of enlightenment—love, acceptance, compassion, and support—operating with peaceful, harmonious thoughts, emotions, and relationships. As we love, respect and support each other, we create golden communities where we live in peace and harmony with others.

Would you like to be involved in creating a golden community? More and more people are interested in creating golden communities, and they are forming all around us. A golden community could be made up of:
◇ Your family.
◇ Your circle of friends.
◇ People you work with.
◇ Your neighbourhood.
◇ Towns and cities.
◇ A global community.

Golden communities are also being built over the internet. Developments in communication systems have made the internet available all around the world, and now almost everyone can become involved in golden communities online. There are now many global meditation groups, conference calls and webinars, all sharing ideas and spreading higher wisdom and understanding.

HOW TO BUILD A GOLDEN COMMUNITY

Building a golden community always starts with one person —

ourselves. As you commit to living your life based on the qualities of enlightenment, you become a beacon of light and an example for others to follow.

Remember, the golden energy is composed of love, acceptance, compassion, peaceful and harmonious thoughts and emotions.

 You have an important role to play in building the golden community all around you.

A person with a higher frequency will always cleanse and dissolve lower energies, raising everything to a higher level. This is the Law of the Universe. Your loving and compassionate presence will influence others and uplift them to a higher frequency and way of life.

Don't be put off by thinking the task is too great. As with your own journey to enlightenment, it is a step-by-step process. Every successful step and progress made contributes to the success of the next step.

A NEW WORLD OF SHARED RESOURCES

Golden communities offer us opportunities to share our resources and contribute our unique gifts and talents.

Can you imagine a world where there is no more hunger? We have all we need on our planet to ensure that everyone's needs are met. We are making progress in this area, albeit slowly, as we still need great change in trade agreements and the way resources are shared.

However, there are many success stories. There are a growing number of pioneering communities who are bringing forward new and inspiring ways of living. Some of these groups store the food they collectively grow in large holding areas and each member of the community can take whatever they need from the store at any time.

THE SPIRIT OF COMMUNITY

I believe wholeheartedly in the spirit of community, with each person contributing their unique gifts, talents and produce for the benefit of the whole, whether they are administrators, gardeners, solicitors, childcarers, poets or writers. No one has to do it all, as each person shares their own unique talents, and they in turn are surrounded by others who share their special gifts.

FLUSH OUT THE OLD — GOLDEN COMMUNITIES CAN THRIVE

Sometimes it seems that progress is moving too slowly, or that we are taking a step backwards. This happens as lower thought forms, habits and ways of operating in the world are brought to the surface to be cleansed.

We can see this happening all around us as inequality and injustice are rampant, so that they can be flushed out of our systems. Of late, all the structures which govern our lives and economies, our leaders, governments, banking systems, and religions, have been in the spotlight across the globe. People are looking for the qualities of honesty, justice, respect and democracy to permeate every area of their lives.

It is important not to get caught up in the turmoil which usually accompanies cleansing, but instead focus on the fact that something better is being created. As we flush out the old, we create a space for the golden light of love and harmony to shine through and create a new, golden community.

Hold a vision of the golden light of love, joy, peace, and understanding uniting all of humanity, so we can live together in harmony and create golden communities all around us.

Golden footsteps

 Let each footstep you take be golden, and leave a trail of love.

A GIFT FOR MOTHER EARTH

You can create pools of light on the surface of Mother Earth with your golden essence.

Can you imagine each footstep you take leaving a golden imprint? As your foot touches the ground, you gift the Earth with your divine essence of love, light and joy.

You can do this wherever you walk during the day. It may be just as you walk along a corridor or up the stairs, or longer distances as you walk to work, do your shopping, or go hill-walking at the weekend.

Health guidelines recommended that we take 10,000 steps per day —an incredible amount of golden footsteps!

Light up the world with golden footsteps as you go about your day.

Rays of divine light

The rays of your divine essence will transform all to love.

You are a powerful being, radiant with light and love. As a service to humanity and our planet, you can send the light of your divine essence ahead of you. Your essence contains rays of divine wisdom, healing, truth and love, and transforms all to loving and harmonious frequencies.

The rays have amazing qualities. They:
◇ Uplift and transform.
◇ Help everyone see situations from the highest perspective and infuse everything with love.
◇ Elevate consciousness, enabling people to act in a higher way.
◇ Help people hold peaceful thoughts and emotions.

HOW TO CREATE RAYS OF DIVINE LIGHT

The rays of divine light are formed from your third eye, throat and heart chakras:

◇ A ray of divine light, wisdom and healing from your third eye.
◇ A ray of divine truth from your throat.
◇ A ray of divine love from your heart.

The three rays meet about a metre in front of you and form into the point of a triangle, which beams rays of divine light ahead of you.

PREPARE YOURSELF BEFORE CREATING RAYS OF DIVINE LIGHT

As the rays of divine light are formed from the light of three of your chakras, it is important to cleanse your chakra column so that your energy can flow freely, containing the highest light.

Flush your whole chakra column with cleansing light. Sense or see your chakras filling with high frequency light and colour, until they are clear, bright and shining with radiant light.

You are then ready to send out rays of divine light to transform all to love.

SERVICE FOR HUMANITY AND OUR PLANET

As you send rays of your divine essence beaming out in front of you, you will be aware of a softening of the energies all around you, as you will also be enfolded in the higher frequency light radiating from the source of your being.

You will know that wherever you are and whatever you are doing, your light is shining brightly, uplifting everyone you meet and transforming all to love.

 The light of your divine essence is like a beam of radiant torch light, lighting up the world.

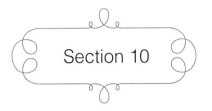

Section 10

Your golden steps to inner peace, happiness and enlightenment

Take the time to review your progress so far, and develop your own personal plan.

You can choose the golden steps to take that will bring you to your destination by following the steps that are most appropriate for you.

Your golden steps

Is there anything stopping you from being an enlightened being today, and living a joyful life of love, abundance, fulfilment, peace and harmony?

This is a very empowering question. It is helpful and energising to take note of the progress you have made so far. Then:

◇   Focus on one or two areas of your life, with the intention of transforming whatever is holding you back.

◇   Choose the sections and golden steps within the book which are most relevant to you, and continue your journey of healing, growth and expansion.

Remember that this journey is taken step by step. As you take each step, the next step that you need to take will become clear. To help you prepare a plan of action, this section contains a summary of each of the golden steps within the book.

SUPPORT FROM YOUR SPIRITUAL TEAM AND EARTHLY FRIENDS

Once you have identified the areas that you most want to work on, enlist your spiritual team to help guide your journey. Also ask your friends to help you stay focused. You can support and encourage each other.

 You will be able to take all of the steps outlined in this book — nothing is beyond what you are capable of doing.

Summary of the golden steps

 You can find inner peace and happiness and reach enlightenment in this lifetime.

LET YOUR DEEPEST WISDOM GUIDE AND INSPIRE YOU

Allow yourself to be guided by your deepest wisdom as you read through the steps below, and choose those which are most relevant to you right now. Then reread the relevant sections within the book; they contain guidance and lots of practical encouragement and suggestions to help you reach your goal.

As you take each transformational step, focus on the next golden step you are drawn to. Allow the words to speak to your heart and soul, and guide you to create the life of your dreams, filled with love, joy, peace, abundance, harmony and fulfilment—all the qualities of enlightenment.

Each golden step you take will move you further along your pathway, drawing your own deep wisdom to the surface, enabling you to remember the magnificence of who you are.

INTRODUCTION TO ENLIGHTENMENT

◊ Recognise who you truly are—a magnificent being, radiant with love, light, joy and vitality. Answer the call of your soul to come back to wholeness again.

◊ How would you feel if you knew that the essence of who you are, the light of your soul, is that of infinite love and light, and that you are already an enlightened being?

◇ Accept your magnificence. Take a few moments to acknowledge the magnificence of who you are. You are a divine being, special beyond words.

◇ Step into the light of infinite possibilities. Sometimes it only takes a reminder of what's possible for you to reach for the transformation and infinite possibilities on offer.

LOVE AND JOY

◇ Love is the key to enlightenment. This includes all its many reflections—compassion, empathy, acceptance, peace, kindness, harmony, and forgiveness.

◇ Love blossoms when we open our hearts and act with harmlessness towards all, with the knowledge that each person is part of the magnificent tapestry of life.

◇ Unconditional love flows from our purest state of consciousness. Open your heart, and love with no conditions or hopes of receiving something in return.

◇ Share the gift of your love. You create a beautiful and enlightened world by sending a stream of love from your heart, touching everyone and everything around you.

◇ Your life can be a joyful experience. Do whatever you find joyous and fulfilling to accelerate your journey to enlightenment.

◇ You are born to experience joy and share happiness with others. When you let go of something holding you back, you create a space for something new to take its place.

◇ You deserve the life of your dreams, and you can make it happen.

◇ Live joyfully. Take many simple steps to add light and sparkle to your day.

LIGHT UP YOUR LIFE

◇ Send blessings and invite divine grace and miracles into your life.

◇ Allow appreciation to open your heart so you can soar with all the good in life and open doorways to higher levels of love, light, peace and joy.

◇ Gratitude opens your heart and attracts even more love and joy into your life.

◇ Give yourself a bright start to your day. A new day is born each morning, full of light, joy and wonderful possibilities. As each day dawns you are offered fresh opportunities to create more love, happiness and fulfilment in your life.

◇ Look for the gift in challenging situations. There is a constant flow of love throughout the Universe. When one door closes, another door opens with a golden opportunity.

◇ Accept that there is a divine plan for your life. Ask that your life unfolds with grace and ease, in a perfect way, and for the highest good of all.

◇ See the best in everyone. Open your heart and enfold everyone you meet with love and acceptance.

◇ Speak to everyone in the language of the Angels—golden words of love, encouragement and support.

◇ Abundance involves all areas of your life, including love, happiness, friendships, peace, health and success. The Universe flows in a natural state of abundance, and you can tap into this energy to make your dreams a reality.

A CONSTANT SOURCE OF LOVE AND SUPPORT

◇ There is a constant source of love and support available to you. You can call on the infinite flow of love throughout the Universe to assist you at any time.

◇ Align with the highest aspect of who you are, your Higher Self, asking to be guided by the highest wisdom and light of your soul.

◇ There are an incredible number of divine beings in service to our Universe, who are willing to step forward to assist you.

Call on your Angels, Guides, Saints and Ascended Masters to help you deal with any challenges in your life, and assist you on your journey to inner peace, happiness and enlightenment.

SPIRITUAL PRACTICE

◊ Give yourself the gift of meditating daily. Still your mind and focus inward, where you can touch into the essence of who you truly are—the light of your soul.

TRANSFORMATION AND SPIRITUAL GROWTH

◊ Step into your power. By transforming whatever is holding you back, and stepping fully into your power, you accelerate your journey to enlightenment.

◊ The greatest gift we can give to others is to be true to ourselves —our happiness is contagious.

◊ Build your self-worth and confidence. Know you are a unique and divine being, perfect from the very first day.

◊ Affirmations will help you transform old habits and patterns, and step into the positive flow of goodness within the Universe, where everything is possible.

◊ Allow the healing light of forgiveness to shine from your heart and transform all to love.

◊ Cut cords and attachments to reclaim your freedom and power. Be prepared to let go of past hurts and trauma, and find healthy and appropriate ways of meeting your needs.

◊ Disconnect from the negative parts of human collective consciousness. You step into your power when you are prepared to reassess your major thoughts, beliefs and behaviours.

◊ You can create miracles of love, joy and freedom in your life when you invoke the cleansing power of the Violet Flame.

HEALING ON ALL LEVELS

◇ There is a miracle of healing constantly happening within your body.

◇ All healing flows from unconditional love. Take whatever steps are necessary to support yourself to heal on all levels—mind, body and spirit.

◇ Take care of yourself with good food, exercise and time to rest. You will feel good, look good and have more energy to enjoy life to the full.

◇ Thoughts are powerful. In every moment you have a choice to hold positive thoughts, thoughts that will serve your highest good and accelerate your journey to enlightenment.

◇ Let your mind be clear and bright and filled with thoughts that nourish you. Take steps to dissolve worries, fears and negative emotions.

◇ Remember the gift of the present moment. The past is in the past, the future has yet to arrive, but the present moment is a gift—it is where you can live your life to the full.

HIGHER HEALING

◇ You can call on higher healing energies to assist you. Ask that you be surrounded by an oval of high frequency light to support you on your journey to enlightenment.

◇ Healing and cleansing your DNA will give you an opportunity to align with the divine blueprint of all your cells, organs and systems and attain a new level of health and vitality.

THE HEALING GIFTS OF NATURE

◇ Mother Nature offers you many gifts to uplift your soul, support your healing, and enhance your well-being.

◇ Rest regularly in the beauty of nature and find balance, clarity and peace.

◊ Love and kindness for all life forms are qualities of enlighten-ment. By living in harmony with the great diversity of life on Mother Earth, you can create a beautiful new world.

◊ Connect with the high frequency light of the dolphins. They will enfold you in their essence of love, joy and bliss, and help you anchor these qualities in your life, accelerating your journey to enlightenment.

LIGHT UP THE WORLD

◊ Offer yourself as an Ambassador for the Light, and spread love, light, peace and harmony all around you. Your presence will be a stream of light, illuminating the way for others.

◊ You can create Heaven here on Earth—your presence makes a big difference. Every act and thought of love has a ripple effect, and contributes to the creation of a bright new golden world.

◊ You can help golden communities thrive. They are built on the qualities of enlightenment—love, acceptance, compassion and support. They operate using peaceful, harmonious thoughts, emotions and relationships.

◊ You can create pools of light on the surface of Mother Earth with your golden essence. Let each footstep you take be golden, and leave a trail of love.

◊ Let the light of your divine essence be like a shining beam, transforming all to love.

Celebrate your successes and welcome the positive changes and new levels of lightness and well-being in your life.

 I wish you many blessings as you take each golden step on your journey.

About the author

Mildred is an international spiritual teacher, and receives many invitations to share her wisdom at workshops and conferences around the globe.

Her vision is to empower people to open their hearts to the lightness and joy of life and step forward into their full potential, creating joyful lives of love, peace, abundance and fulfilment.

She is the founder of 'Wisdom of the Heart', a School of Enlightenment and Sacred Sound Healing. She is also a Principal Teacher of the Diana Cooper Foundation, an international school of light-workers.

Mildred has had opportunities to study with many great teachers, both in Ireland and abroad, which started her on her own teaching and mentoring career.

She also has a passion for healing with sacred sound. She holds many inspirational workshops and training programmes, which focus on empowering students to support their health and well-being with sound, and become sound healing practitioners.

Mildred has also set up many workshops, talks and online courses to spread the messages within this book and support the reader.

Mildred has recorded many CDs including 'Angel Light and Guidance', 'Dolphins and Unicorns—Helping us Create Heaven on Earth', and 'Sacred Sound—Temple of Healing and Rejuvenation'.

Mildred firmly believes that we are at the dawning of a new Golden Age of Enlightenment, where we have wonderful opportunities to live in a higher frequency of unconditional love, creating Heaven on Earth. To help spread a golden light throughout the world, Mildred donates 10% of fees from every course to organisations which work to enhance the lives of others and relieve suffering.

For more information on her schedule, or to subscribe to her free newsletter, please visit www.mildredryan.com.

Gratitude

I offer heartfelt thanks to the Angels, Saints and Ascended Masters for the love, light, guidance and wisdom I received as I wrote this book.

Also I am hugely grateful to my family for taking care of my dog and house for many months so that I could go on retreat to complete my work.

Thank you Michelle, David, your lovely family and two wonderful dogs, for providing a special sanctuary for me to do my writing—the seaside cottage, nestled in the beauty of nature in the west of Ireland. The early morning and sunset swims were truly fantastic, allied with the many walks along coastal pathways. Nurtured by the clear fresh air with the scent of the ocean, it was the perfect location to be inspired.